Special Praise for
The Wisdom of a Meaningful Life

"In *The Wisdom of a Meaningful Life*, John Bruna sheds clear light on the difference between hedonic pleasure and genuine well-being. While Albert Einstein compares the pursuit of the former to the ambitions of a pig, the Dalai Lama suggests the cultivation of the latter is the very meaning of life itself. On this basis, the author brings a rich ethical and transformative context to mindfulness meditation, couching it within the framework of a meaningful worldview, set of values, and way of life. I highly recommend this timely and insightful book."

B. Alan Wallace, PhD
Buddhist teacher, scholar, and Director of the Santa
Barbara Institute for Consciousness Studies
Author of *The Attention Revolution* and *Mind in the Balance*

"*The Wisdom of a Meaningful Life* is an easy-to-digest guide on how to create the causes for bringing about genuine happiness and true contentment in life. The premise of John Bruna's book is that all human beings face similar challenges in life, and we all strive for genuine happiness. John operationalizes what it means to be truly happy. He helps the reader learn how to approach choosing a meaningful set of values, laying a solid foundation, and setting one's motivation to take action. Although there are hundreds of books and journal articles written about it, John describes mindfulness as a way of living, and breaks down its components in a meaningful way that we can all relate to. I highly recommend John's book because it offers a complete package that any- and everyone can relate to regardless of your background, socioeconomic status, profession, ethnicity, race, religion, or gender."

Seth Shaffer, PsyD
Founder/President of Harmony Through Education

"*The Wisdom of a Meaningful Life* is a powerful meeting of ancient Buddhist teachings and humble stories of one man's journey through a life of recovery and Buddhist practice. I have read and recommended many introductory books on mindfulness over the years, but this one will go to the top of my list of recommendations, for its clarity and honesty, and its emphasis on a whole and wise approach to one's life."

Zenshin Florence Caplow, Soto Zen priest and teacher
Unitarian Universalist minister, author of *The Hidden Lamp:*
Stories from Twenty-Five Centuries of Awakened Women

"John Bruna is a masterful communicator who uses the day-to-day examples from his and our lives to invite us to consider 'what is a meaningful life for us?' Who better to be our guide in this exploration than a man who was once challenged by hardships in his own life? *The Wisdom of a Meaningful Life* is a practical guide for those trying to understand what this mindfulness stuff is all about and what you might do to begin practicing it. He helps us to understand the foundations of mindfulness so we can begin to practice living meaningfully, no matter where the starting line is in our learning."

Mark Molony, MSW
Therapist, coach, and cofounder of the Mindful Life Program

"John Bruna's kind, loving presence is infused in these pages where he shares many tools along with simply stated wisdom that guides us to a more meaningful life of contented happiness. From his years as a Buddhist monk and in recovery, John has gained the insight and clarity to offer deep wisdom in clear accessible language. He is a skilled communicator, committed in word and deed to helping others find the path to true freedom and transformational living. John is a natural storyteller and this book resonates with his big heart, authenticity, and humor."

Peter Kuhn
Buddhist priest, ordained by Thich Nhat Hanh
Twelve-step Buddhist workshop, group, and
retreat facilitator; writer; and jazz musician

"Simply written and yet profound, *The Wisdom of a Meaningful Life* is a practical and accessible guide to cultivating a healthy mind. This book brings clarity to concepts that have been both overused and misused in popular literature. John Bruna's work is enduring and brilliant!"

Rebecca A. Willow, EdD, LPC, NCC
Associate Professor, Gannon University
Clinical Mental Health Counseling Program,
Department of Psychology and Counseling

"In all the buzz about mindfulness these days, it is deeply refreshing to find a book that sets the topic firmly within a context of values and wisdom, and thus closer to its Buddhist origins. Its pages are rich with practical insights that have been forged in the fires of Bruna's own self-inquiry rather than plucked in the pleasant gardens of philosophy. Bruna delivers his message with friendly and encouraging clarity—that a meaningful life is not the result of lessons and guidelines dutifully applied, but the natural outcome of a life well-lived."

Rebecca Novick
Author of *Fundamentals of Tibetan Buddhism*

"In this inspiring and practical book, John Bruna shows us how to truly build a more meaningful and fulfilling life. Bridging the gap between scientific and spiritual study, *The Wisdom of a Meaningful Life* goes far beyond the typical mindfulness primer and teaches us how to use these tools to completely transform our lives."

Stefan Bate, MA, LAC
Executive Director, A New Path

"In *The Wisdom of a Meaningful Life*, John Bruna proclaims the simple, if not elusive, truth: You are the master of your own happiness. With skill, personal insight, and loads of practical wisdom he shows us how to stop waiting for outer circumstances to make us happy and empower ourselves to create truly fulfilling and meaningful lives."

Chris Lemig
Tibetan Buddhist Monk
Author of *The Narrow Way: A Memoir of Coming Out, Getting Clean, and Finding Buddha*

The WISDOM of a
MEANINGFUL LIFE

The WISDOM of a
MEANINGFUL LIFE

The Essence of Mindfulness

JOHN BRUNA

CENTRAL RECOVERY PRESS

LAS VEGAS

Central Recovery Press (CRP) is committed to publishing exceptional materials addressing addiction treatment, recovery, and behavioral healthcare topics, including original and quality books, audio/visual communications, and web-based new media. Through a diverse selection of titles, we seek to contribute a broad range of unique resources for professionals, recovering individuals and their families, and the general public.

For more information, visit www.centralrecoverypress.com.

Publisher: Central Recovery Press
             3321 N. Buffalo Drive
             Las Vegas, NV 89129

21 20 19 18 17   2 3 4 5

Library of Congress Cataloging-in-Publication Data

Names: Bruna, John, author.
Title: The wisdom of a meaningful life : the essence of mindfulness / John
   Bruna.
Description: Las Vegas, NV : Central Recovery Press, 2016.
Identifiers: LCCN 2016008944 (print) | LCCN 2016016491 (ebook) | ISBN
   9781942094180 (paperback) | ISBN 9781942094197
Subjects: LCSH: Peace of mind. | Mindfulness (Psychology) | Meditation. |
   Conduct of life. | Happiness. | BISAC: SELF-HELP / Personal Growth /
   Happiness. | BODY, MIND & SPIRIT / Meditation. | RELIGION / Buddhism /
   Theravada. | BODY, MIND & SPIRIT / Healing / General.
Classification: LCC BF637.P3 B78 2016 (print) | LCC BF637.P3 (ebook) | DDC
   158.1--dc23
LC record available at https://lccn.loc.gov/2016008944

Photo of John Bruna by Jeffrey S. Rose. Used with permission.

Cover design and interior design and layout by Deb Tremper, Six Penny Graphics

DEDICATION

This book is dedicated to you, the reader. It is my heartfelt aspiration that this book provides you with inspiration and tools to improve the quality of your life, empowering you to more skillfully live in alignment with your deepest values and develop your highest potentials. It is also my hope that as you do so, you share your happiness and wisdom with your family, friends, community, and all those you encounter.

ACKNOWLEDGMENTS

It is with deep gratitude that I would like to acknowledge and thank all of the precious teachers, friends, family, and strangers who have helped me throughout my life. It is really the wisdom and inspiration I was fortunate enough to glean from them that made this book possible.

In particular, I would like to thank my dear friend, Sue Adolphson Rose; my amazing wife, Laura Bartels; and my insightful editor at Central Recovery Press, Dan Mager, for the time, energy, and talent they provided in helping to edit this book. Their insights and wisdom conspired to bring the wisdom of my teachers to life in a clear, engaging, and accessible way.

I would also like to thank my precious daughters, Jessica Rose and Virginia Monahan, for helping me become a better father, as well as all of my students at Jordan High School for inspiring me to become a better human being.

It is my humble aspiration that you find this book helpful and that it provides you with clear, practical wisdom and tools to cultivate genuine happiness by engaging in a life you find meaningful.

TABLE OF CONTENTS

CHAPTER ONE
The Search for Happiness

"The search for happiness is one of the chief sources of unhappiness." ERIC HOFFER

It is a universal truth that all beings seek happiness and try to avoid suffering. This is a primary and fundamental motivation for us all. Yet, more often than not, genuine happiness eludes us, while suffering—anxiety, stress, worry, depression, fear—pervades our lives.

All too often, the very quest for happiness becomes the source of our suffering. This dynamic plays out again and again in our daily lives. The things we think will bring us happiness: a good job, a loving relationship, good health, a nice house, a reliable car, quality recreation, a rewarding social life, become the cause of our stress, worries, and concerns.

How is this possible?

We live in a time of incredible abundance and luxury. We have the ability to moderate the temperature of our homes, summon the collective knowledge of the world on our phones, access entertainment at the touch of a button, and even adjust the firmness of our beds. Yet, despite all the creature comforts available to us, it seems we have more mental, emotional, and physical problems than ever.

At the core of these problems is an increasing level of stress in our lives. Stress does not simply make us feel bad and take an emotional toll on us, it actually affects our physical health as well. Numerous studies have found that prolonged stress appears to adversely affect our immune system and can increase the risk of heart disease, diabetes, depression, gastrointestinal ailments, asthma, and Alzheimer's disease. We all know from personal experience that stress can rob us of our happiness during the day and even prevent us from getting rest at night. When we search for the source of our stress, we find that it is related to our work, relationships, health, and quality of life—again, the very things we believe will bring us happiness.

In reflecting upon and examining this phenomenon over the past thirty years through my own experience in recovery from addiction and my work helping others as a counselor, educator, and spiritual advisor, I have come to understand that, like a bad country song, we are usually looking for happiness in all the wrong places. We are trying to find it in people and things that ultimately cannot provide it and are largely out of our control. The best people, things, and circumstances can offer us is temporary pleasure. They can never provide lasting happiness.

But that is where we put our energy with the hope that if we can just line everything up correctly, we will be happy. We do this even though we *know* people (including ourselves) with good jobs, great relationships, prime health, lots of toys, and time for leisure are still subject to depression, anxiety, fear, worry, anger, frustration, and disappointment.

How is it that we continually fall into this trap?

One explanation can be found in the groundbreaking work of Harvard psychologist Dan Gilbert, PhD. He explains that although our minds are exceptional and perform many functions extremely well, our faulty perceptions and cognitive biases can lead us to imagine the future inaccurately, particularly what will make us happy. He describes an "impact bias" that causes us to consistently misjudge how happy some things will make us and how unhappy other things will make us.

In his TED talk "The Surprising Science of Happiness," Dr. Gilbert describes how field work and laboratory studies have shown that significant events, such as winning or losing an election, gaining or losing a romantic partner, getting or not getting a promotion, passing or not passing a college test, have a much smaller, less intense effect on us, and a much shorter duration, than we expect. He also cites research on major life trauma and happiness, which suggests that three months after such events, with few exceptions, there is no effect at all on a person's happiness. This flies in the face of the most basic beliefs and assumptions that underlie many of the choices we make in our lives.

In a recent major shift in psychology from a primary focus on mental health problems to studying mental health and well-being, universities and researchers are now dedicating time and resources to studying the science of happiness, compassion, and altruism, among other related topics. The frequent area of focus is the cause(s) of happiness and the search for scientific answers to explain why some people are happier than others, even when they face similar life circumstances.

One of the most popular models coming out of this research states that outside circumstances in life are responsible for only 10 percent of our happiness.[1] Yet, even with 90 percent of our happiness attributed to other factors, we are putting most of our energy into improving our circumstances.

According to this model, 50 percent of happiness is genetically determined. This is often referred to as our "set point." You'll notice that some people tend to be more pessimistic than others, and some people tend to be naturally happier and more optimistic. When things happen in our lives that we feel good about, we are happy for a little while then come back to our set point. Likewise, when things are challenging and create problems or stress, that too, passes and we again return to our set

---

1   Sonja Lyubomirsky, Kennon M. Sheldon, and David Schkade, "Pursuing Happiness: The Architecture of Sustainable Change," *Review of General Psychology* 9, No. 2 (2005):111–31, doi: 10.1037/1089-2680.9.2.111.

point. Reflect on your own life, and you will see this to be true. Life has its ups and downs, but our basic level of happiness over time seems to be pretty steady.

The final 40 percent of happiness is attributed to intentional activity such as thoughts, actions, and behaviors.[2]

So, according to this model, instead of just striving to improve the outer circumstances of our lives, it is much more important to look at how we think about, respond to, and interact with the people, events, and circumstances we encounter.

Another important recent discovery is the plasticity of the brain. Neuroscientific research has demonstrated that we can create new neural pathways and actually change our brain with intentional activities. Understanding this, if we are able to use our thoughts and actions consciously, we can rewire our brain and even change our genetic set point. In this way, we can directly affect 90 percent of the causes of our happiness—instead of seeking to better our circumstances, which affects only 10 percent.

While I find these new scientific developments interesting and insightful, I believe they only confirm the time-honored universal wisdom about the true source of happiness. The key to genuine happiness has never been a mystery; in fact, it can be found again and again in ancient wisdom, philosophy, contemporary psychology, our grandparents, and in the lessons we have been taught since childhood. In Plato's *Euthydemus*, Socrates establishes clearly that happiness does not depend on external things, but on how they are used. Or as my Little League coach told me, "It is not whether you win or lose that matters, it is how you play the game." Regarding our inner peace, well-being, and genuine happiness, what matters most is not what we have in life, but how we live it.

---

2   Sonja Lyubomirsky, Kennon M. Sheldon, and David Schkade, "Pursuing Happiness: The Architecture of Sustainable Change," *Review of General Psychology* 9, No. 2 (2005):111–31, doi: 10.1037/1089-2680.9.2.111.

It is important to remember our circumstances are constantly changing and that they offer far less joy or suffering then we imagine they will. Though our circumstances, people, and the world we live in is always changing, there is something constant that we can depend upon: when we do things we feel good about, we naturally feel good about ourselves. This is a key point to understand and incorporate in our lives— our genuine happiness comes from doing things we feel good about, not from doing things that make us feel good.

Of course, there is nothing wrong with doing things that make us feel good; the point is that we will feel good only as long as the activity lasts. When we do things that we feel good about, we create a deeper and more lasting sense of well-being, inner peace, and happiness. Whenever we reflect on that situation, we have a sense of worth, value, and integrity.

It is actually a simple, straightforward, and measurable truth: When our actions are in alignment with our values and beneficial to ourselves and others, we feel better. As true and as simple as this is, it is extremely challenging to accomplish.

It is my hope this book will provide the tools and resources needed to reduce, if not eliminate, harmful mental afflictions and cultivate a deep sense of inner peace, well-being, and genuine happiness by living a life based in truth, aligned with your values, and beneficial to others. The way to achieve this is to learn to live mindfully.

These days, mindfulness has become popular in the mainstream, giving rise to a variety of evidence-based methods for reducing stress and improving quality of life. Simple mindfulness practices can help us become more present in the current moments of our lives, which reduces mental rumination on past events and worry about possible future ones.

Through these techniques, we discover most of the worries, fears, and concerns that dominate our lives are not actually present in the current moment. They exist only in our mind, and our untrained mind is constantly producing thoughts that take our attention away from what is happening now. Understanding this and being able to develop the skills to bring us back to the present moment allow us to find more calm and balance in our everyday lives.

However, this is not enough to truly transform our lives. Mindfulness is much more than present-moment awareness. It includes and facilitates the cultivation of concentration, wisdom, and the ability to make healthy choices that lead to genuine happiness and a meaningful life. Mindfulness is not an isolated skill; it is a practice embedded in a rich context of teachings and trainings focused on freeing us from suffering. The essence of this practice is encompassed by four areas: attention, values, wisdom, and open-heartedness.

1. **Attention.** We begin developing our attention by establishing a daily meditation practice. In this way we start training the mind to be present and attend to what we choose, instead of having it constantly drag us around. In order to live a meaningful life we need to be present in our life.

2. **Values.** Values are a critical component of mindfulness but, unfortunately, this is left out of many current mindfulness teachings. The source of finding inner peace, genuine happiness, and well-being is living a life that is in alignment with one's values and is of benefit to oneself, others, and the greater good.

3. **Wisdom.** As we begin to increase our attention through meditation, we are more able to consciously bring awareness into our daily activities. We can start observing ourselves, others, and the world—more accurately recognizing unhealthy habits, tendencies, biases, projections, and emotional triggers in our lives. With this level of awareness, we realize the impermanent nature of emotions, thoughts, events, and identify the true sources of our suffering, as well as the true sources of our happiness and well-being.

4. **Open-Heartedness.** By cultivating the four immeasurable attitudes of equanimity, loving-kindness, compassion, and empathetic joy we consciously water the flowers instead of

the weeds in our thoughts and actions. When we cultivate equanimity, loving-kindness, compassion, and empathetic joy in our hearts and minds, we grow the antidotes to attachment and aversion, hatred, ill will, and jealousy.

This book will provide you with a comprehensive approach to living mindfully so that you can live your life consciously, with attention and intention, cultivate genuine happiness, and create a meaningful life. It is a culmination of the wisdom of many teachers I've had the great benefit of learning from and training with over the last thirty years. These lessons have empowered me to live mindfully, transforming my life, and giving me the honor of helping others transform theirs.

I was once a young man filled with fear, insecurity, shame, and hopelessness. My early life was filled with anger, violence, and substance abuse. Even though, in my heart, I always wanted to be a good person, I wound up hurting everyone close to me. My best efforts led me to homelessness and having the mother of my daughter take her away from me because I was not a fit parent.

Fortunately, in the midst of great suffering I had a moment of clarity that changed my life. It was an undeniable realization and reached me at the very core of my being. Not simply an understanding or revelation, but an irreversible, intrinsic knowing. Like all great truths, it was something I had learned many times before but never truly understood. Quite simply, it was that all of my suffering was not caused by others, my environment, or how I was raised. My suffering came from how I lived my life. There was no one to blame but me.

At the same time, I realized my happiness was also dependent on how I lived my life. This was much more than knowledge or intellectual understanding of a philosophical view; it was a direct realization of that truth. For the first time in a long while I experienced a rising sense of hope that I could change and be able to lead a meaningful life.

That was in August of 1984. From that moment on, I gave up alcohol and other drugs and began the journey to transform my life.

I started to participate in twelve-step programs, which taught me the value of helping others. Ultimately, it was in these programs that I learned one of the most valuable questions that would shape my journey: Instead of asking "How can I feel good?" I was taught to ask "How can I help?"

Until then, my life had been focused on me—I was the center of the universe. Whatever circumstances, choices, or opportunities presented themselves, my concern was how it would affect me. This new perspective allowed me to get out of myself and truly engage with others. I found whenever I asked how I could help, I was empowered to improve, not only the quality of the lives around me, but my own as well. Instead of focusing on my circumstances, I started focusing on my intentional activities.

From that point on, whatever work I did, I tried to be as helpful and beneficial as possible. I was far from perfect and still am. I made, and continue to make, mistakes. However, just as a lump of coal can become a diamond over time, with that attitude, my job delivering auto parts turned into a management position. The shy, insecure, and awkward young man who used to live under a bridge then became a substance abuse counselor working with adolescents and families, a teacher working in a low-income minority high school, a father and grandfather, and a Buddhist monk.

I have had the rare opportunity to live in many different social and economic environments. I've been homeless and owned a home; I've been a dishwasher, an auto mechanic, and a corporate manager; I have lived in communities riddled with drugs and violence and in spiritual communities grounded in love and kindness.

Throughout all of these experiences, I have had the good fortune of encountering wonderful teachers whose lives embody their teachings. I have learned that regardless of outer circumstances all human beings share similar problems.

And I have seen there are proven, time-tested solutions to our problems that can empower all of us to cultivate our highest potentials.

CHAPTER TWO
Genuine Happiness

"Happiness is a state of inner fulfillment, not the gratification of inexhaustible desires for outward things." VENERABLE MATTHIEU RICARD

If we are looking for happiness in our lives, it is important to understand the difference between stimulus-driven pleasure and genuine happiness. Confusion related to these two concepts is at the core of many of our mental and emotional problems.

Stimulus-driven pleasure comes from the world around us. It requires a stimulus—a delicious meal, an award, a vacation, a concert—that provides a pleasurable experience. The pleasure is dependent on the stimulus. Or, in other words, the pleasure depends on outside circumstances.

The "good" feelings that are triggered from these circumstances are only temporary, and the stimuli do not consistently produce the same result. The same stimulus can trigger varying levels of pleasure and also create suffering. For instance, if you eat too much of the delicious meal or listen to your favorite song too many times, what was pleasurable can turn into a painful experience. At the same time, not getting your favorite meal when it was expected or having a vacation canceled leads to temporary suffering.

To be clear, there is no problem with savoring a delicious meal, having a nice vacation, or enjoying a concert. The problem lies in our unrealistic expectations that these experiences will provide more, or longer-lasting, happiness than they can. When we reflect on our lives, we find we have had numerous wonderful experiences, but we are still subject to stress, worries, sadness, fear, and anger. We can have the vacation of a lifetime, and a week later we are upset. Yet, in spite of this reality, our minds continue to tell us that if we can arrange enough pleasurable experiences in our lives, we will be happy.

One obvious problem is that we don't have much control over the outer circumstances in our lives. While we can influence some of the factors in our lives, ultimately, we don't have control over the economy, other drivers on the road, our friends, relationships, the weather, accidents, or even our own physical health. Another problem is that it is not actually the stimulus that provides the pleasure; it is how we *perceive* the stimulus. We can be on a beautiful vacation and feel miserable, or we can simply sit in our front yard and feel quite content. Our mental, emotional, and physical health have a direct effect on the degree of pleasure or pain we experience during any activity in which we participate. Despite this, we focus on external circumstances instead of *how* we are taking part in them.

Genuine happiness is not dependent upon a stimulus or having things go our way. It does not come from the world; it comes from what we bring to the world. It is related to our intentional activities. The term "genuine happiness" is used frequently by eminent Buddhist teachers and scholars such as B. Alan Wallace and the Venerable Matthieu Ricard, to describe the Greek term eudaimonia. Eudaimonia, an important subject of the ancient Greek philosophers, is a deep serenity and inner well-being based in virtue. When I use the term genuine happiness, or eudaimonia, it is different than the mere transient pleasurable experiences we often call happiness. It is a state of inner flourishing and well-being capable of including and transcending all of our emotional states and experiences. It represents not just the waves of our emotional experiences, but the ocean itself.

To use a common analogy, genuine happiness is like the depths of the ocean. The waves on top of the ocean represent the emotional ups and downs of life that come and go. They are transient, just as our feelings and circumstance are. They can be turbulent, calm, or somewhere in-between. Meanwhile, the depths of the ocean remain calm, connected to the waves but not caught up in them. In other words, genuine happiness is a deep sense of well-being and contentment that is available even in difficult times. The cultivation of genuine happiness does not mean we don't feel emotions, such as sadness. Instead, it allows us to experience sadness without being caught up in it, thus avoiding feelings of hopelessness or despair. Genuine happiness is a well we can draw upon to sustain us through difficult times, and it allows us to flourish even in the simplest of activities.

The way we cultivate genuine happiness is not by collecting a long list of pleasurable experiences. It comes from within us. It is an inside job. It is cultivated by making healthy choices that are based in reality, in alignment with our values, and beneficial to others. In essence, we cultivate our genuine happiness by living a meaningful life. When we participate in life in a way we feel good about, in alignment with our values, we find inner peace regardless of the outcome or external circumstances. Conversely, when our actions violate our personal values we don't feel good about ourselves, regardless of the outcome or circumstances.

Understanding this, we know it is not the external situations and outcomes that matter most in life; it is how we live our lives. It is not the house that brings us happiness; it's how we came to get the house and what we do in it. It is not the job that creates happiness; it's how we participate in the job and what we do with our work. It is not the relationship that makes us genuinely happy; it's how we participate in that relationship. It is not making a lot of money that creates happiness; it's how we make the money and what we do with it.

This is not to say that stimulus-driven pleasure is harmful or something to avoid. It is perfectly normal and healthy to seek pleasurable experiences and enjoy them. As I mentioned earlier, the problem does not lie in the experiences themselves; it lies in our *unrealistic expectations* that these experiences will provide a much greater level of happiness—or, for that matter, unhappiness—than they actually do.

If we understand that the events, activities, relationships, and circumstances of our lives will consistently give rise to only temporary experiences that are both pleasant and unpleasant, then we are free to enjoy the pleasurable ones while they last, and we are able to more effectively deal with the difficult ones. We need to understand the limits of the effects our outer experiences have and not confuse them with the source of genuine happiness.

The key distinction that determines whether an activity is simply a stimulus-driven pleasure or a cause of genuine happiness is the motivations and attitudes we bring to it. There is a subtle but important difference between doing something we feel good about and doing something that makes us feel good.

If we understand this distinction, we are able to transform all of our experiences, whether pleasurable or difficult, into opportunities to cultivate genuine lasting happiness. When our actions are in alignment with our values and beneficial to others and to ourselves, then we are doing things we feel good about.

Such meaningful activities are the essential ingredients of a meaningful life. Every time we reflect on these activities, we can feel good about our participation in them, and this gives us a deeper sense of value and well-being. On the other hand, if we participate in activities solely to seek pleasure for ourselves, without a deeper motivation tied to our values or living with purpose and meaning, then we will find our satisfaction is limited and fleeting. This applies to all of our experiences, whether they are painful, pleasurable, or somewhere in between.

For example, in 2006, my mother was dying in a hospital in Southern California. It was a difficult and challenging time for all of the members of my family. Though clearly I am biased, I can honestly say that my mother was an amazing and virtuous woman. My father passed away when I was only six and my mom was left to raise nine children alone. We did not have much money, but she always found a way to ensure our needs were met and let us know that we were loved. My mother endured incredible hardships, including the death of my sister in an automobile accident not long after the passing of my father. She worked full time, rode the bus, took night courses, and raised all of us. She had an incredible reservoir of compassion and inner strength, as well as a deep commitment to helping others. Throughout her life, my mother was a living example of virtuous activity. She was one of those rare people who had friends of all ages and backgrounds.

My mother had entered the hospital for a surgery and there were complications. Though we did not know it at the time, she would not leave the hospital alive. In the days and weeks after the surgery, there were times of hope and improvement, as well as setbacks and despair regarding her recovery. It was a difficult and challenging time for all of the members of my family.

However, as painful as it was for all of us, it is one of the experiences I can look back on and view as a time I was able to cultivate genuine happiness. I say this because, although this was a time of tragedy for our family, we were all able to be there for our mother, and for each other. We set up a schedule, taking shifts so she had one of us with her twenty-four hours a day. As her time came to an end, we were all able to be with her at her bedside. Before she passed, we were able to tell her she had done a good job with us and that we were all okay—this is what mothers worry about the most; they worry about their kids. We let her know that it was okay for her to go, and that we were grateful for everything she had done for us.

Although I feel tears beginning to flow and I am flooded with the emotion as I write this, I can tell you that being able to participate in her last hours in such a beneficial way was one of the most meaningful experiences of my life. It has contributed greatly to my well-being. Every time I reflect upon it, I am grateful for the way my family and I were able to be there for her, as well as for each other. While we all felt the sadness and loss that is a natural part of grieving, feelings of connection, gratitude, and warmth also enveloped this experience.

Consciously paying attention to our intention is the skill that allows us to transform our everyday experiences into meaningful ones. This is not just true of difficult situations, but also those that are pleasurable or even neutral. Any activity we consciously engage in with attention and intention is an opportunity to cultivate our highest potential. The key is to be accurately aware of our motivation.

Something as simple as having friends over for a meal can have different effects on us based on our motivation and engagement in the activity. Let's look at two different motivations:

1. We are motivated to have friends over because we value them. We invite them over and, with love, prepare a meal for them we hope they will find delicious and nourishing.
2. We are motivated to have friends over to impress them with our cooking skills. We invite them over for a meal and hope they will enjoy it while seeing us as amazing in the kitchen.

In the first case, if our values include friendship, connection, generosity, and making others happy, our meal is clearly in alignment with our values, and the meal becomes a meaningful experience on multiple levels that creates a lasting sense of well-being. Even if the meal is overcooked or does not turn out the way we had hoped, we can still share an evening together that meets the goal of expressing how much we value the friendships.

However, if we carry over the same values to the second scenario, we will find our motivation—to have others see us as good cooks, seeking their validation and praise—conflicts with those values. So, even if we value generosity and making others happy, the motivation here is ultimately to make us happy by having others see us as valuable, skilled, and so on. If they enjoy the meal and compliment us, we will experience a temporary feeling of happiness. This happiness is stimulus-driven—contingent upon the meal being delicious and others viewing and responding to us positively. If the meal goes poorly, it can create disappointment and dissatisfaction in us. This up-and-down cycle of temporary moments of pleasure and pain, contingent upon outside circumstances, can change dramatically if we learn to consciously pay attention to our motivations and align our actions with our values.

Unfortunately, most of us live our lives unconsciously, busily going from one thing to the next without reflecting on our motivations, values, and the deeper meaning of our lives. Living this way leaves us vulnerable to letting normal ups and downs trigger a wide range of temporary emotional experiences, both pleasant and unpleasant, which dominate our lives.

All too often, we wind up *reacting* to the challenges and opportunities in our lives instead of *responding* to them with clarity and wisdom. When we react, it is usually an unconscious action arising from and colored by an emotion such as fear, surprise, anger, or joy. As I will discuss later, when we're caught up in an emotion it is difficult to see events clearly, often causing us to be reactive. To use a common analogy, it is a lot like trying to rearrange the deck chairs on the Titanic to make it as comfortable as possible instead of focusing on turning the ship in the direction of safety. We are able to find temporary pleasures here and there, but unable to direct our lives in a way that is most meaningful.

We can develop the ability to overcome our reactive tendencies with mindfulness. When we are mindful, we are able to recognize our emotions being triggered and not get caught up in them. We can pause, bring awareness into the moment, and reflect upon the most beneficial way to respond, both in the moment and in the long-term. In this way, we empower ourselves to make conscious choices that cultivate lasting well-being for ourselves and others.

Another model we can use to illustrate how easy it is to fall into the trap of confusing short-term, stimulus-driven pleasure with genuine happiness is the Eight Worldly Concerns. The Eight Worldly Concerns is a Buddhist teaching that illustrates how our preoccupation with temporary happiness actually creates more long-term suffering. Although it stems from Buddhist philosophy, this is a universal teaching that clearly applies to all of us. If we examine them closely, we find these are primary motivating factors, either consciously or unconsciously, in nearly everything we do. They are:

- **Gain and loss**: We are happy when we get what we want and not happy when we lose things or people we like. Thus, we spend a lot of time and energy trying to get what we want and avoid losing what we have.

- **Pleasure and pain**: It is quite natural that we enjoy pleasurable experiences and want to avoid pain. Usually, from the moment we get out of bed in the morning, we are trying to find and engage in pleasurable activities and avoid painful ones.

- **Praise and criticism**: We like it when people praise us and we don't like it when people criticize us. On subtle levels, we spend a lot of time seeking validation from others and avoiding their displeasure.

- **Good reputation and bad reputation** (also called fame and insignificance): We want people to think highly of us, and we don't feel good when others think ill of us or believe we don't have much to offer.

Having these motivations is normal and not a problem in and of itself. There's nothing wrong with seeking the things we need and trying to avoid losing them, seeking pleasure and avoiding pain, appreciating validation from others, and having a good reputation. The problem comes when we allow these temporary concerns to override our long-term well-being and happiness. Because such worldly concerns are stimulus driven, they are temporary and, rather than cultivate meaning, they often create worry, rumination, and unnecessary suffering when we allow them to be our primary guiding motivation. As with all stimulus-driven pleasures and pains, we need to remember their limitations.

The problem is, over time, we have become so habituated by these worldly concerns that they become our default motivations. We constantly make decisions and engage in activities with them as our primary concern without factoring in or reflecting on our values. In the quest to get what we want, be accepted by others, or just feel good, we often go against our own values in ways so subtle that we aren't even aware of them. When we are in alignment with our values, we do the right thing regardless of gain or loss, pain or pleasure, praise or criticism, good or bad reputation, and we feel much better about ourselves.

What others think about us is not nearly as important as what we think about ourselves. It is important to bring reflection and wisdom into our choices. If we value honesty, it is important to tell our boss or our friends the truth when we make a mistake, regardless of worldly concerns. If we constantly try to avoid pain or challenges, we wind up creating bigger problems.

It's often healthy to deal with a difficult situation, endure a little pain, or put off pleasure for a beneficial long-term result. We teach our children about delayed gratification, yet forget to apply it in our own lives. Rather than reacting to feelings and desires that arise, it's important to take a moment to reflect on making healthy choices that contribute to a durable lasting well-being and a life we define as meaningful.

CHAPTER THREE
The Unruly Mind

"If you can change your mind, you can change your life." WILLIAM JAMES

One of the most important realizations I have come to over the past thirty years—the essence of the inspiration for this book—is that most people, given the opportunity to reflect, already know how to improve the quality of their lives.

When I taught high school, my students could easily make a list of five things they could do to improve their lives. Yet, despite being able to make such a list, most of those students (like the vast majority of people in this world) were unable to follow through and actually do the things they listed. I'm sure all of us can relate to this. We are all aware of some simple things we could do to improve the quality of our lives right now and, for some reason, we don't do them.

Recognizing this dynamic challenged me to ask one of the most important questions of my life: What is it that prevents me from doing the things I know are healthy and beneficial? If I valued honesty, why did I lie? If I wanted to help people, why did I hurt them? If I wanted to be healthy, why did I do unhealthy things?

It turns out that I was not unique. The inability to answer these questions is a nearly universal problem, affecting almost all human beings. One of our biggest problems is that we rarely ever ask ourselves where the resistance to being the person we want to be comes from. The primary obstacle preventing us from being able to make healthy and productive changes in our own lives is not our circumstances, nor a lack of knowledge about what to do, it is our untrained mind. We have untrained minds that are conditioned by our experiences, habits, and tendencies and are constantly producing thoughts and emotions that draw our attention away from being present and able to make wise choices.

The best explanation of this phenomenon that I have found comes from one of the scholars I mentioned earlier, B. Alan Wallace, who calls it obsessive compulsive delusional disorder. This is not a disorder you will find in the *Diagnostic and Statistical Manual of Mental Disorders* (DSM); rather, it is a pervasive condition of the mind that nearly everyone has.

The first point Wallace makes is that the mind is obsessive in its constant production of thoughts, images, emotions, and desires. This is easy to verify; just try to keep your mind free from thoughts for a minute or two, and watch what happens. When we try this, we notice something quite remarkable: We are not consciously producing the thoughts that arise; our minds are producing them—regardless of our conscious desire to have them or not. What's more, much of the time we are not even conscious of all the thoughts and images that are steadily flowing through the space of our minds.

Secondly, with this obsessive stream of thoughts running through our minds, our attention is compulsively drawn toward those thoughts. Instead of being present in our current moments, our minds are diverted to past events or future concerns. If we make a conscious decision to simply sit and relax and be present, very soon we will observe this compulsive activity of the mind. Within moments, our attention will turn to plans, memories, fears, or desires. We quickly realize our minds have much more control over our attention than we do.

This strikes at the root of our problem. We have little conscious control of our attention. If we are to establish any free will in our lives, we need to be able to direct our attention where we would like it to go, rather than have our unruly mind dictate what we think about.

A clear example of this is worry. We may be aware of a potential future concern that creates worry. Intellectually, we can understand that worrying about this problem won't affect its outcome, and we might realize there is nothing to worry about at this time. Yet, despite our conscious decision to not worry, we find the mind continues to bring our attention to the potential problem and create worry. We can tell the mind there is nothing to worry about, and the mind will answer, "Oh, yes there is!"

If we take a moment to observe the mind, its obsessive and compulsive nature is apparent. A consequence of it dragging us from one thought to another—whether a past event, future concern, or mere distraction—is we are not even present for most of our daily activities. Do any of these statements sound familiar?

"Have you seen my car keys? I don't know where they are."

"I just had that piece of paper a moment ago, and now I can't find it."

"Where did I put my glasses?"

"What did I come in here for?" (after walking into a room)

And, one of my personal favorites:

"What were we just talking about?"

We believe we forgot where we put our car keys, what we did with the paper, or what we are talking about. While this may be true on some level, the more accurate explanation is that our minds were somewhere else when we put down the keys or that piece of paper, and we were not even listening to our own conversation. Our attention was pulled away by our obsessive-compulsive minds. Even when we consciously decide to do some task during the day, we may forget all about it as our minds get caught up in other thoughts and activities.

Many studies have shown that simply having a distracted mind negatively affects our well-being. A Harvard study, published in the journal *Science*, conducted by Matthew Killingsworth and Daniel Gilbert, found that almost half of the time people's minds were wandering, and their thoughts were not related to what they were doing. It also found that people were happiest when their thoughts and actions were aligned. Their level of well-being, though impacted, actually had less to do with what they were doing or thinking about and more to do with their mental presence, matching their thoughts with their actions.[3]

According to this study and many others, mind-wandering (thinking about things that distract us from what we are doing), whether it involves pleasant or unpleasant thoughts, leads to less happiness than being attentive to what we are doing, even if it is just raking the yard. Mind-wandering should not be confused with consciously and intentionally allowing one's mind to rest or daydream. Mind-wandering is a research term that is the opposite of presence of mind. Just having presence of mind increases our level of happiness.

In addition to being distracted, the mind rarely sees the world accurately. Based on our conditioning, biases, attention level, and current emotional and physical states, the mind projects distorted qualities, characteristics, and judgments onto the people, places, and events in our lives. Ultimately, this is the main cause of our mental and emotional suffering, and our inability to cultivate genuine happiness. The untamed mind, influenced by our emotional and mental biases, prevents us from seeing things clearly and making healthy choices based on reality.

Most of the time, the mind is quite delusional. By delusional, I don't mean the psychotic-level loss of contact with reality described in certain forms of serious mental illness or psychiatric disturbance. In this context, delusional refers to phenomena that are much more common to our everyday experience.

3 Matthew Killingsworh and Daniel Gilbert, "A Wandering Mind is an Unhappy Mind,"
   Science, 330, No. 6006 (November 2010): 932, doi: 10.1126/science.1192439.

One of my favorite examples of everyday delusion is the idea of the annoying person. We all know someone who is annoying, right? In truth, there is no such thing as an annoying person. However, the mind can quickly point to the people we find annoying and label them "annoying people." As soon as we see one of these people, we can experience intense feelings and become annoyed. The person doesn't even have to say or do a thing.

Now, if this person actually was annoying, wouldn't everyone find him annoying all the time? Yet, the same person we find annoying, others find interesting. In fact, for some entirely unexplainable reason, someone might even want to marry this person! When we look at people like this more accurately, we find they are not intrinsically annoying; rather, we are annoyed by something they say or do.

If we look even deeper, we often find we are not really annoyed at all; we are merely experiencing the feelings of being annoyed, which are temporary. The feeling of being annoyed will leave, and we will still be here. The people we think of as annoying do and say things all day long that we would not find annoying. They are probably not annoying when they walk their kids to school, take out the trash, cook a meal, pay their bills, help their parents, or just sit at home watching TV. In fact, during most of their day, we would not find them annoying.

The true cause of our irritation is not the other person; it is our judgment and perception of that person. Being annoyed is a mental experience, and the cause of a mental experience is the mind. The delusion is the belief that the other person is truly annoying and he or she is the actual cause of our feeling annoyed. If we take a moment to reflect, we can recall times when we were feeling great and people we normally found annoying didn't bother us at all. We can also recall times when we were tired or irritable, and even our best friends annoyed us.

The belief that our happiness or sadness comes from other people or events is one of the most pervasive everyday delusions. Our happiness or sadness actually comes from how we perceive and respond to those people and events. Let's look at two ways of relating and responding when our car won't start:

1. **Delusional and reactive:** We think our car should always start and not be subject to breaking down. We may become angry, upset, or panicked, quickly calling to mind our bad luck and asking, "Why me?" The mind presents us with how terrible this is, possibly looking for who is to blame—maybe our mechanic, our partner, or the car manufacturer. We ruminate on how inconvenient this is, how much money this could cost, and what a bad day this has turned out to be. Eventually, we do make an alternative plan to get where we're going and have the car fixed. However, we may carry our frustration and perceived bad luck throughout our day, sharing it with our friends.

2. **Realistic and responsive:** Understanding it is natural that cars sometimes don't start (there is a whole industry based on the reality that cars break down: the automotive repair industry), after a moment of surprise, we accept and assess the situation, and move into solution mode. We get a jump-start or other needed help if available, or we make an alternate plan to get where we are going. We then make a plan to get the car fixed. Instead of asking, "Why me?" and thinking of our bad luck, we have the perspective that this is just an everyday event, and we might even be grateful we have a car and a place to go when so many others do not. Instead of letting this ruin our day, it reminds us of the resources and opportunities we have.

In both of these scenarios, the event is the same, but the outcome and the amount of suffering are very different because of the perspective and attitude we brought to the situation. It is a common practice—and a complete misunderstanding—to blame our mental and emotional suffering on other people, events, or things when the true source is our own mind. It obsessively and compulsively draws our attention away from the current moment, preventing us from seeing clearly with perspective, and projecting unrealistic expectations and exaggerated qualities onto the people and events in our lives.

This is not to say there are not tragic and painful experiences we all have in our lives that will naturally give rise to feelings of emotional suffering. This is a normal and intrinsic part of our human experience. The point here is that there is an excessive amount of mental and emotional suffering we endure that is unnecessary. It can be avoided if we understand more clearly the true sources of both our suffering and our happiness. The good news is that we can tame our unruly minds, cultivate wisdom, and learn to cultivate genuine happiness as we live in the real world. We do this by learning to live mindfully.

The tools of mindfulness empower us to be aware of our thoughts, feelings, and environment with clarity and discernment. Mindfulness enables us to distinguish healthy tendencies from unhealthy ones, beneficial habits from harmful ones, and delusional grasping from clear understanding. It allows us to make choices that are healthy, helpful, and aligned with our values. In so doing, we cultivate inner peace, genuine happiness, and a meaningful life.

CHAPTER FOUR

Attention

"But it is extremely important to check and see if whatever meditation we do is an actual remedy for our suffering." LAMA YESHE

The first step—and one of the key components to living mindfully—is learning how to tame the unruly mind and cultivate attentional balance. In other words, we must learn how to direct our attention where we want it and hold it there. Ultimately, this is the only way to establish free will in our lives.

It is a common myth that we have such free will and use it daily. As described in the previous chapter, most of our choices and reactions are triggered by an unruly mind based on distorted perceptions; they are not conscious choices based in reality. If we are to have free will in our lives, we have to be fully available to make the choice. This means we need to be present in the current moment with clarity and wisdom. Instead of having the mind drag us around from one thought or feeling to the next, we need to train the mind to serve us in the healthiest way possible.

If we observe the mind, we will notice that it tends to be either overly active—ruminating, planning, reminiscing (often referred to as "monkey mind")—or tired, such as when we can't muster the energy to pay attention. These two states are often described as excitation and laxity. The mind tends to be either too excited or too lax. Rarely is it relaxed, stable, and attentive.

This dual tendency toward excitation and laxity has been noted in many wisdom traditions throughout time. Most people just get used to it and accept is as a normal state of mind. However, it is *not* our normal or natural state of mind. The natural state of the mind is blissful and luminous. In fact, when the mind is calm and clear at the same time, it returns to its natural state and happiness spontaneously arises. Unfortunately, the obsessive, compulsive, and delusional activities of the mind obscure its true natural state. This state is verifiable. It has been consistently replicated by meditators over thousands of years, yet it eludes the vast majority of us. When we are able to cultivate attentional balance, avoid getting caught up in excitation or laxity, and develop the ability to focus our attention in a relaxed, stable, and clear way, only then will we discover this natural state of mind.

The method of cultivating attentional balance that has been refined over thousands of years is available to us in *shamatha* meditation. Shamatha means calm or peaceful abiding. This practice was developed to cultivate concentration, calm the turbulent mind, and abide in its natural state. This specific meditation practice is the antidote to the most detrimental mental affliction we have: the obsessive and compulsive mind. But before I begin to unveil this method further, let me say a few words about meditation.

First, the form of meditation I am suggesting is simple and can be done by anyone. You do not need to climb a mountain, sit in full lotus position, or learn any complicated visualizations. It is as simple as learning to relax your body, breathe naturally, and pay attention. Second, there are many different types of meditation, and all of them are designed with a specific purpose in mind. The great teachers of all meditation traditions emphasize that it does not matter so much whether we sit this way or that way, do this meditation or that meditation; what matters is whether our meditation counteracts our mental afflictions.

This is an extremely important point, and one I believe is frequently overlooked. So often we hear studies indicating that meditation has all sorts of wonderful benefits. Beautiful posters tell us that if we all meditated the world would be a peaceful place. Unfortunately, these claims are often out of context and not entirely true.

Meditation can have a beneficial, non-beneficial, or neutral effect on us. We can use meditation to escape the responsibilities and challenges of life, or to face them. We can use meditation to concentrate all our energy on selfish means, or on helping others. We can do elaborate meditations working with energy and, without proper guidance, actually damage our bodies. We can also use certain meditations, understanding their specific purpose and with guidance from a qualified teacher, that enable us to alleviate, if not eliminate, mental and physical afflictions, and improve our quality of life.

So remember: When learning to meditate it is important to understand the purpose of the meditation, the directions of the meditation, and how it addresses our afflictions. The shamatha meditation I suggest is very safe, easy to learn, and can be extremely effective in cultivating attentional balance.

Because many of us do not have a great deal of freedom and time to participate in hours of training, practice, and meditation, it is important to use what little time we do have to meditate in the most effective way. Most people I've taught over the years are fortunate if they have thirty minutes a day to dedicate to formal meditation practice. We lead very busy lives, and it can be challenging to break old habits and create the time for a meditation practice.

So, if you are able to meditate for only ten, twenty, or thirty minutes, why not choose the meditation that directly counteracts our biggest obstacle, the unruly mind? That is the specific purpose of shamatha meditation practice. Developing a regular shamatha practice will even improve the quality of your other meditation practices, as is provides a greater level of mental stability for them.

Meditation practices are divided into two categories: concentration and contemplative/analytical. Shamatha is a concentration practice. The unique feature of shamatha meditation is that we focus all of our attention on one object to the exclusion of all else. No matter what else arises, whether it be delicious thoughts, blissful feelings, or an itch, we maintain our attention on the chosen object of our meditation, such as the breath. In this way, we are able to train the mind to attend to what we choose, rather than have it drag our attention around. This meditation practice is also extremely healthy for our bodies. It allows us to rest body and mind in their natural states, which is very healing.

An added bonus to all of these benefits is that shamatha is a simple and straightforward practice that anyone can learn. It has three stages of development: relaxation, stability, and vividness. It is often explained using a tree as a metaphor.

The roots of the tree represent relaxation. For us to truly progress in this practice, we need to relax the body while keeping the mind alert. As simple as this sounds, it is a skill to be cultivated. Rarely is the body physically relaxed while the mind is clear and mentally alert. We notice that when we relax, we have a tendency to feel tired or even fall asleep. Most of the time, the nervous system is quite active and ramped up. So, initially, our practice is simply learning how to relax our bodies without falling asleep. This is the root of our tree.

As we develop in our practice and are able to be alert while relaxed, what will become the trunk of our tree—stability—begins to sprout. Stability occurs when we are able to maintain our attention on our chosen object of meditation. If we have a consistent practice, even if it is only a short time daily, we will learn to have a relaxed body and an alert mind that is eventually able to remain focused on what we have chosen to attend to. This is a gradual process; trying to rush it does not help.

At first, the mind will wander, and wander again, many times, challenging us to maintain stability. At this point, many people struggle and begin to believe they are not capable of meditating. However, this is when we are actually making progress! If the mind wanders 1,000 times during meditation and we bring it back 1,000 times, we have just had 1,000 mindful moments that we would not have had otherwise. Every time we notice the mind has wandered, we become mindful and are able to direct it back consciously. This is the process of training the mind.

Most of the time, when the mind wanders, we are not aware of it; it simply takes us along for the ride. But gradually, with consistent practice, the trunk of stability will develop, and we will be able to rest our awareness on our chosen object for longer periods of time.

Eventually, this will lead to a high degree of clarity and vividness; these are the leaves of our tree. There is a sequence: First relaxation, then stability and, finally, vividness. Of course, in our goal-oriented modern Western world, we often try to reach for the leaves first, before we have developed healthy roots and a strong trunk. Rather than being beneficial, this actually hinders our progress. Patience and consistent practice, without attachment to a goal, will be much more productive. As Mother Teresa noted, "Without patience, we will learn less in life. We will see less. We will feel less. We will hear less."

Over the years, I have learned there are two primary reasons we struggle to develop a consistent meditation practice. First, we don't really know *why* we are meditating. We have a vague idea that it is good for us—we have heard and read about its benefits, and we believe it will bring us inner peace. Then we try different styles of meditations with hope that we will find something. However, because we don't know the specific qualities of the meditation we're doing and how it is targeted to specific afflictions, it is difficult for us to see any progress, and our practice fades away. Establishing any new habit is challenging; to be successful, we have to have a clear, realistic goal and a measurable path by which to arrive at that goal.

As we prepare to meditate, I like to remind people to take a little time to remember why we are meditating: to call to mind that this is an opportunity to develop ourselves fully and cultivate a meaningful life with attention and intention. By choosing to meditate, we are developing the ability to direct the mind and attention where we choose, to live consciously, to stop falling victim to every thought, feeling, worry, or desire that pops into our heads. We give ourselves permission to relax and nourish ourselves, allowing body and mind to heal. These experiences become resources we can draw upon.

Second, we try to do too much too soon. It is much better to start with short meditations of good quality than long meditations of poor quality. Quality is much more important than quantity here. When we begin a meditation practice, it is best to choose a short one and learn to do it well. Venerable Thubten Chodron states that the best meditation practice occurs when we finish and feel as if we could have done a bit more. This encourages us to look forward to our next session rather than seeing it as a chore, which we might do after a painfully long session.

I began my practice many years ago with ten minutes a day. At the time, I was a poster child for monkey mind, and ten minutes seemed like an eternity. But, eventually, ten minutes became very comfortable, so I tried fifteen. Before long, fifteen minutes became twenty, became thirty, and so on, until my meditation had transformed from awkward effort to precious opportunity.

SHAMATHA MEDITATION PRACTICE USING THE BREATH AS THE OBJECT

Be seated in a comfortable position with your back straight in a chair, on a meditation bench, or on a cushion. The key is to be comfortable enough so you can be physically relaxed and won't have to move. The more you can still your body, the easier it will be to still your mind. While there are many reasons to have a straight back, the most practical one in this meditation practice is to allow your abdomen to rise and fall easily and naturally. It is also beneficial to have your tongue lightly touch the roof of your mouth. This allows saliva to flow more naturally, so you have less need to swallow. It is ideal, but not necessary to breathe through you nose. If you cannot breathe through your nose for some reason, it is perfectly okay to breathe through your mouth.

Decide on a length of time for your meditation. It is best to use a timer so checking the clock will not distract you. Once the timer is set, take a few moments to allow your awareness to descend into your body and simply become aware of what feels solid about your body. Let your awareness rest in the solidity of your body, starting where your body comes in contact with the chair, cushion, bench, or floor. Then expand your awareness throughout your body and rest it in the solidity of your body—what feels solid.

After resting your awareness in the solidity of your body, do a body scan to relax and release any tension you may have. I suggest bringing all of your awareness to the crown of your head and letting it rest there for a few moments. Then let your awareness slowly flow down, relaxing and releasing any tension you find along the way. I like to visualize my awareness as a soothing balm that melts away any tension it comes in contact with. Let your awareness flow from the crown of your head, across your forehead, relaxing and releasing any tension there. Relax the areas around your eyes, relax your jaw, and continue to relax the various parts of your body, all the way down to your toes.

The intention is to relax your body while learning to keep your mind alert. There is no rush; simply take your time and relax as you bring your awareness throughout your whole body. Once your body is relaxed, take a moment to give yourself permission to let go of all worries and concerns; give yourself permission to relax, breathe, and nourish yourself. In essence, allow yourself to be here now and to meditate.

Next, bring all of your awareness to the tactile sensations of the breath as it enters and exits your body. Allow your breathing to be natural and unmodified. Don't try to breathe deeply and don't worry if you breathe softly. Just let the breath do what it wants and observe it. You might begin by observing the sensations of the full length of the breath, or you might choose a target area such as the rising and falling abdomen or the breath as it goes in and out of the nostrils, resting your awareness there. Whatever your chosen target of focus, rest your attention there and be aware of each breath as it enters and exits your body.

If you notice your mind wandering, just relax, release the thoughts, and return your awareness to the breath. Every time you notice your mind wandering, this is actually a success. If you notice your mind wanders a thousand times, then you just had a thousand mindful moments! Normally we don't even notice when our mind wanders and simply go along for the ride. Another method that many people find useful to help focus attention during this meditation is counting the breaths. Choose a low number (I suggest between seven and ten), then try to be fully aware of each breath up to the designated number. If your number is ten, try to be fully aware—mindful—of ten consecutive breaths. If you lose count, go back to zero and begin again. If you achieve ten mindful breaths, reward yourself with ten more. Continue this process until your timer rings. After practicing consistently over a period of time (that varies from one person to another), most people find they are able to let go of the counting and simply rest their awareness on the breath.

Developing a Successful Meditation Practice

Here are some suggestions that can help you be successful in establishing your meditation practice. While you are encouraged to explore and find what works best for you, these are tips that are commonly offered by meditation teachers and I have found to be beneficial for many people.

1. If possible, **designate a regular space for your meditation**. Ideally, the space will be away from your work area. Make it warm and inviting, and decorate it with images or items that are inspirational or meaningful to you.

2. **Set aside a regular time for your practice.** Many people find that morning is best, before the day gets too busy and active. Starting the day with meditation gives you some quality time to cultivate your attention and set your intention for the rest of it.

3. **Set your intention to meditate.** The best time to do this is before going to sleep the night before. As you set your alarm clock, call to mind the benefits of waking up early and meditating. Set a strong intention to wake up at a particular time and see yourself getting out of bed to begin your practice. This is much more successful than just setting an alarm, waking up, and then trying to find the motivation to roll out of bed and meditate. I visualize myself getting out of bed, walking down the hallway to the coffee pot, pouring my coffee, and walking upstairs to my meditation room.

4. **Do your best to meditate every day.** If you wake up late or have only a little time, meditate for a shorter period. Even a few minutes will help maintain your connection to the value of your practice. That said, don't beat yourself up for not meditating. I find it is much more helpful to have a positive and rewarding relationship with my meditation. I give myself credit for just having the *desire* to meditate. This keeps my practice nourishing, rather than a chore. If you miss a day, it is not the end of the world—or your practice. It is an opportunity to be kind to yourself and to bring that kindness into your day as you participate with others. In fact, meditation is only a small part of a mindfulness practice. The bulk of your practice is in how you live your life.

CHAPTER FIVE

Values

*"I am not bound to win, but I am bound to be true. I
am not bound to succeed, but I am bound to live up
to what light I have."* ABRAHAM LINCOLN

As we develop our attention and mindfulness, we will begin to be able
to direct our attention more consciously. Now comes a very important
question: Where do I direct my attention? Or to put it another way, what
should I be mindful of? While mindfulness is often thought of simply as
present-moment awareness, it also refers to a state of "non-forgetfulness."
This refers to the ability to keep our awareness on the chosen object of
our attention. As we engage in daily life, what is it that we should not
forget as we pay attention in the present moment? What do we get most
distracted from throughout the hustle and bustle of our days? In our
quest to find pleasure and avoid suffering, what is the biggest obstacle?

I would submit there are many things that are critical to keep in mind,
that we should not let fall away from our awareness as we engage in the
moments of our lives. Not the least of these is the impermanent nature
of our lives and the lives of all those around us. Maintaining awareness of
this truth can inspire us to engage in the moments of our lives in the most

meaningful of ways, preventing us from wasting precious years. How much of our lives have we already wasted, lost in worry, stress, laziness, rumination, or in activities that prove to have no real value and that we might even regret at the end of life?

If we are able to come to terms with the simple truth that our time is limited, we have the opportunity to ask ourselves some most important questions:

- What is a meaningful life?
- How would we like to live this day that will never come again?
- What is more important than asking ourselves what is important?

It has always intrigued me that we so rarely ask these questions. It seems as if we reserve them for times of crisis or tragedy, when things are falling apart around us or when we've lost a loved one. But why wait? We can bring these questions into our lives each and every day.

I believe the most important question we can ask ourselves every single day is *How can I make this day meaningful.*

At the time of our death, what will matter most is how we lived our lives. Every moment, every breath, is a new opportunity to let go of the past and become the person we choose to be. However, this opportunity is available to us only if we are aware of it—and if we are aware of the person we want to be. We need to learn to be constantly aware of the moments we are in and the opportunities they offer. This is why using meditation to tame our obsessive-compulsive mind and develop our attention is so important. We want to be present in the moment, mindfully aware of our internal and external experiences and how our perceptions color them. We also need to maintain awareness of the person we want to be, the qualities and habits we would like to develop in ourselves, as well as the ones we would like to eliminate.

As expressed by Nāgasena, a Buddhist sage who lived around 150 BCE, " . . . mindfulness, when it arises, follows the courses of beneficial and unbeneficial tendencies: these tendencies are beneficial, these unbeneficial; these tendencies are helpful, these unhelpful." If we are going to live a meaningful life, we need to explore, investigate, and discover what that means to us. This is something we need to bring to our mind again and again, in all of our activities and throughout our days. Otherwise, it falls to the wayside as we get busy with our daily activities. To intentionally develop ourselves and live a purposeful life requires some personal time of reflection, as well as ongoing, mindful observation of our activities and experiences. The guiding principle here is that genuine happiness is cultivated when we are able to engage in life in ways that are meaningful to us and in alignment with our values.

But to live a life that is in alignment with our values, we need to know what those values are. When was the last time you explored your values? This is not something we commonly do unless a significant event compels us to look deeply at the meaning of our lives. When I teach mindfulness courses, one of the first things I do is provide the participants with a long list of values and ask them to select six that are most important to them. Exploring our values always turns out to be a rewarding experience.

One thing we usually discover during this process is that some of our values have changed over time. As we live our lives and gain new experiences, some values become less important while others become more so. We also find that on different days or at different times certain values are more pertinent. This is another reason why it is a good idea to consistently check in and reflect upon what is truly important to us. Even for people whose values seem steadfast, withstanding the test of time and experience, it is still helpful to engage in the exercise of values clarification.

Universally, in the therapeutic, spiritual, and educational groups I have participated in over the years, I have found that people consistently find a source of strength and inspiration in their values. When things are falling apart and life gets challenging, our values and purpose in life are always available to sustain us, and even transform our greatest challenges into opportunities for personal and spiritual growth. Unfortunately, too often we lose sight of our values and their significance in our lives.

In my early recovery, I had a small studio apartment and a job at an auto parts store. It did not pay much and I had to scrape to be able to make ends meet. Even getting enough to eat was challenging. I bought hotdogs to cook and sell to the other employees who in turn paid for my meal. I really loved that job and the people I worked with. I was grateful for the opportunity and the training it gave me.

One of my coworkers gave me the chance to purchase his car on credit. At that time I did not have a car and took the bus to work. It was a 1969 green, four-door Plymouth Satellite. I remember it well. It was in great shape and everything, even down to the interior lights, worked. He was selling it to me for $500. I was able to give him a down payment and make payments until it was paid off. I was thrilled to finally have a car and drove home filled with joy.

Unfortunately, about a week after I got the car my mother's car broke down. It was going to require another engine and she did not have the money to repair it. My sister lived with my mother and used the car to get her daughters to school. Without hesitation I offered them the use of my car until they could afford another engine. Initially, this did not feel like an effort at all, rather I found it extremely rewarding to be able to help. For so much of my life, I was not in a position to be able to help and now I was. The ability to be of service in a way that was clearly in alignment with my values provided me with a sense of self-worth.

As things turned out, it was quite a while before my mother and sister were able to afford to fix their car. In the meantime, I was back on the bus. I was once again limited in the places that I could go, and back to carrying groceries home from the store. Over time my sense of self-worth started to turn into self-pity. I had finally gotten a car, paid it off, and then was not able to use it.

This all came to a head one day as I was once again standing at the bus stop in the rain. I was taking the bus to work in the early morning, cold and wet. My mind turned to a wonderful rendition of poor me. Poor me, I have to ride a bus. Poor me, I don't get to drive my own car. Poor me, life is so unfair. As I was beginning to really settle in to a deep state of self-pity, the bus stopped and let on a passenger. As she got on the bus I noticed that she was blind. In an instant, poor me lost all meaning. This woman also *had* to take the bus. She would *never* be able to drive her own car. Yes, life is unfair, and instantly I became grateful for the overwhelming gifts and opportunities I had in my life.

In my self-pity, I lost track of my values and all perspective of the gifts and opportunities I have received in my life. This precious woman reminded me of how truly fortunate I was and brought me back to reality. The car I thought would bring me happiness had become the source of my sorrow. The joy that arose from my generosity had turned into self-pity. I've never forgotten that moment and can still tell you the corner of the bus stop: Santa Anita Avenue and Huntington Drive in Arcadia, California. I did not talk to her, but to this day I'm grateful for her lesson and carry her in my heart as one of my teachers.

That invaluable lesson gave me the strength to stick to the values of generosity and family that had prompted me to loan my car in the first place. Eventually, my mother and sister were able to get their car fixed and I was once more behind the wheel of my 1969 green, four-door Plymouth Satellite—this time much wiser, with gratitude and a stronger sense of self-worth and inner peace.

In order to live a meaningful life, we need to maintain an awareness of what is meaningful to us and what our values are. Otherwise there is no way for those values to factor into the decisions we make in our lives. Without awareness of our values, we revert to our unconscious default settings of the eight worldly concerns and simply focus on trying to find temporary pleasure and avoid pain.

A list of values is included in the Appendix in the back of this book, and I encourage you to take some time and reflect upon them, identifying some of the more prominent values that you would like to guide your life.

Let's take a look at honesty, one of the values that comes up frequently for many people. If this is one of your core values, take time to reflect upon its importance in your life and how much it guides, or does not guide, your decision-making process. In reflecting upon its importance in your life, you might ask yourself the following questions:

- What does honesty mean to me?
- Does this mean honesty in all things?
- What about self-honesty?
- Does honesty require telling everyone exactly what I think?
- Why is honesty so important to me?
- What are the benefits of being honest?
- What are the pitfalls of being dishonest?
- How do I feel about myself when I'm honest or dishonest?
- How do I feel when others are honest or dishonest with me?
- How honest am I with myself and others in my daily life?
- How does honesty relate to authenticity in my life?
- Does my honesty extend to admitting my mistakes?
- Does my honesty extend to paying my taxes?
- What are some of the examples in my life when I chose to be honest even though it was difficult?
- What are some examples in my life when I chose to be dishonest because it seemed easier at the time?
- How did these things turn out for me?

You can use these questions or create similar ones for any of the values you find important. After taking time to clarify and reflect upon some of your core values, the next step is to be mindful of them in your daily activities.

A good way to start is to choose one value and set an intention to bring it to mind as much as possible throughout the day. Then see how often it can guide your actions or how often the value can be swept aside in your decision-making process. It is good to have a journal, notepad, or just a piece of paper to write down your intention and the discoveries you make throughout the day regarding this value and your ability to incorporate it into your daily activities.

This is an invaluable method to gain insight into yourself and the world around you. In this way, you can become a more engaged participant in your own life. Instead of simply going along for the ride—moving from one activity to the next, being dragged from one thought to another, changing from one emotion to a new one—you can develop the ability to consciously choose which activities you will participate in, decide whether to indulge or dismiss your thoughts, and select responses to your emotions that are both intentional and more beneficial for you and those around you. In just one day, you will come to some important realizations and experience a real difference in your level of engagement in your life.

You will also find this requires effort and can be quite challenging. While it is actually a simple process based on universal wisdom of the ages, it can be difficult to master. If it were easy, there would be no need for this book. Developing inner wisdom, learning healthy habits, and living a purposeful life don't just happen; these things come from reflection, self-examination, and conscious action.

As you become aware of your core values, begin to learn to keep them in mind, and intentionally bring them into your daily activities, you will become increasingly aware of the habits, tendencies, and beliefs that interfere with living in alignment with your values. This is the beginning of true wisdom: identifying within yourself that which prevents you from being who you really want to be.

What are the habits, tendencies, and misperceptions that, in the guise of finding pleasure and acceptance, actually bring about suffering and isolation? The only way to remove these is to recognize and understand them. To do that, we need to be conscious of how these things arise and prevent us from living the life we find valuable and meaningful.

There are many subtle ways in which we compromise our values, often without a second thought. For example, have you ever been late to something because you overslept? I imagine most of us have. How often have we made up another reason to explain why we were late? Was it easier to tell the truth to the friends who knew us and would understand? Did we feel we needed to make up something out of concern over what others might think of us? Was this a valid concern, or was it about being attached to our pride and self-esteem? Was there a potential negative consequence we wanted to avoid? What would have happened if we had simply told the truth? Do we hold on to the belief that others don't oversleep and that this represents some flaw in ourselves? What is at the core of the fear that did not allow us to tell the truth? Is it valid?

There are a lot of answers to these questions, and we all do things for a variety of motivations. Our biggest problem is not that we make mistakes or don't always live up to our values; it is that we are often completely unaware of the reasons why we fall short of our intent to live up to our values.

To harness the full resources and benefits of living mindfully requires more than training our attention to be present without the elaborations and projections of our unruly mind. It also requires the ability to maintain awareness—a state of non-forgetfulness—of our intentions, tendencies, values, and the insight we acquire from engaging in our lives consciously. In this way, we are able to identify and nourish the habits and tendencies we find beneficial, and start eliminating the ones preventing us from living our lives meaningfully.

CHAPTER SIX
Wisdom

"My grandfather of mindfulness must watch constantly after this spoiled child of deluded mind to save him from disaster." THINLEY NORBU RINPOCHE

Mindfulness is an insight practice facilitating self-awareness and empowering us to see and engage in the world more accurately. The more accurately we see and experience the world, the easier it is to avoid unnecessary stress, worries, and fears arising from our unruly and busy mind. When we are able to bring conscious attention to our thoughts, emotions, and activities, we can directly experience how they affect us and our perception of the world around us. This is the way we cultivate wisdom and enhance our ability to make healthy choices and participate in meaningful activities.

In the absence of mindful self-awareness, we do not usually question the thoughts, feelings, and stories our mind presents to us in our daily activities—we usually accept them as truth. We tend to perceive the world outside of ourselves as a concrete, objective place, and that our experiences of it are accurate. However, if we bring awareness and perspective into our daily life, we find the world we experience is actually subjective and relational. In other words, how we perceive the world has a lot to do with us: our attitude, how we feel that day, whether we are tired or not, how we were raised, our culture, and our previous experiences.

One simple way to understand this process is to reflect upon times when our mental and physical states have affected our experiences:

- When we are not feeling well, we may find the thought of our favorite meal makes our stomach queasy.
- When we are feeling sad, our favorite activities can't bring us joy.
- When we are tired and irritable, our best friend can seem annoying.
- When we are healthy and happy, people we dislike don't seem to bother us.
- If we're not in a hurry, traffic may not be stressful.
- If we are in a hurry, traffic seems unbearable.

These are just a few simple examples that are easy to recognize. However, it is important to understand that the same dynamic applies to virtually everything we experience. The events, people, and circumstances in our lives are never intrinsically all good, bad, or mediocre on their own. We can enjoy or dislike the same activity on different days. We may love and hate the same person at different times. We can find the same job fulfilling and unfulfilling over time. The problem is that we believe the activity itself is absolutely fun or horrible, the person is wonderful or terrible, and the job itself is rewarding or unrewarding. Because of this misperception, we keep focusing on our outer circumstances instead of our relationship to them.

Worse yet, we believe this is how the world actually is. For example, if we have a bad experience in a restaurant, we believe it to be a terrible restaurant and tell our friends not to go there, believing their experience will be the same—because that's the way it is. We don't consider that maybe our server was having a challenging day and that normally he or she is quite wonderful. We don't consider the possibility that the particular dish we had was not reflective of the restaurant as a whole. We don't even consider that our friends might enjoy meals we don't.

Likewise, if we enjoy a meal and have a great time with our server, we highly recommend the restaurant and believe that all our friends will have the same experience. However, they may go, have a long wait for a table, possibly have a another server, a meal cooked by a different chef, and have a very different experience than we did. Whenever the thought of that restaurant appears in our mind, we have a specific judgment that it is terrible or wonderful.

The other interesting thing is that our view of the restaurant remains the same over time. Even if the last time we went to a restaurant was two years ago, we still think of that restaurant in terms of that experience without considering that it may have changed over time. Our view becomes stagnant even though things are continually changing, including ourselves.

How about apple pie? Do you like apple pie? I happen to love apple pie and have a dear friend who bakes the most delicious apple pie I've ever had. When I eat it, I think that apple pie is truly delicious. But is that true? Where is the deliciousness? Is it in the apple pie? If it were in the apple pie, then everyone would find that apple pie delicious. As hard as it is for me to imagine, there are actually some people who don't like apple pie and would not find it delicious at all. My mind tells me the apple pie itself is the source of the deliciousness, but in truth, I am having an experience of deliciousness as I eat the apple pie. Someone else eating the same apple pie may not enjoy it nearly as much as I do. And, as pointed out earlier, if I weren't feeling well, perhaps due to a stomach flu, that apple pie would not be delicious to me either.

Let's talk about strawberries for a moment. I love strawberries and have always thought they are a healthy food for me. Is that true? I would think most of us could agree that, generally, strawberries, in moderation, are healthy for us. But what if someone is allergic to them? I have a dear friend, Louise, who was allergic to strawberries so it was not healthy for her to eat them. Even if you are allergic to strawberries at one point in your life and they are bad for you, at another point in your life you may not be allergic and they will be quite wonderful. This is true of my friend, who can now enjoy strawberries.

What about your favorite drink? We can spend quite a bit of money buying, or time and effort creating, our favorite drink. When we taste it, it is refreshing and delicious. Again, that drink, which we enjoy so much, might be disliked by others. I personally think of coffee as precious, radiant nectar. However, (believe it or not!) some people don't like coffee at all. We may also notice that on a hot day after some exercise, a cool glass of plain water provides just as much refreshing deliciousness as our favorite drink.

The same principle applies to many aspects of our life. For instance, when we say we've had a terrible day, we might ask: In relation to what? Compared to someone who's homeless? When we say we've had a wonderful day, ask again: In relation to what? Compared to someone finding their long-lost parent? What some people call a great day, others would find quite mediocre. What some people call a terrible day, others would love to have. Our "worst" day could be someone else's "best" day.

When we step back from any particular situation, we can see the situation itself is never intrinsically all good or all bad. Our perception of it is dependent upon many factors, including our perspective, attitude, and physical and mental state at the time. If we change any of these factors, our experience changes.

These examples illustrate again and again that the world we experience is subjective and relational, rather than objective and quantifiable. Many of the qualities we attribute to our outer circumstances are not intrinsic to them. *We* are always a part of the equation. Because we don't recognize this, we often create a lot of our own mental and emotional suffering. We keep trying to change the circumstances instead of our relationship to them.

One of the most common ways we misperceive reality is in how we judge and label other people. Earlier, I used the example of an annoying person to illustrate how we can mislabel someone and attribute the quality "annoying" as intrinsic to that person. Let's expand upon this a bit with someone we label "a jerk." Let's call him Jimmy.

At some point, Jimmy did something, or a few things, we did not like, which reflected the qualities of a jerk. So we identify Jimmy as a jerk. Every time we see Jimmy, what do we see? We see a jerk. As soon as we see him, tense feelings arise, possibly even anger, irritability, or resentment. Even if Jimmy doesn't do anything but enter the room or just pass by, our mental and emotional state is affected. We are not even open to the possibility that Jimmy might have some positive things to contribute to any situation in which we encounter him. Even if we see Jimmy doing something wonderful, like making a contribution to a charitable cause, we might think he's only doing it to look good. We don't attribute any kind or generous qualities to him.

I would propose that in most of his daily activities Jimmy is actually not a jerk. Is he a jerk when he's waking up and getting his day started? Is he a jerk when he's cooking breakfast? Is he a jerk when he's getting his kids dressed for school? Is he a jerk when he's paying his bills? Is he a jerk when he is buying his mom a birthday gift?

You can see the point. Throughout his daily activities, most of the time Jimmy is doing a variety of things with a variety of different motives— just like all of us. At various times he is helpful, thoughtful, selfish, kind, angry, nervous, or fearful. I'm pretty sure that at no point in his life did he wake up and decide that he wanted to be a jerk. Yet despite this, every time we see Jimmy our mind labels him as a jerk, and this colors all of our interactions with him. Because of this, we are unable to be open and available to the possibility that Jimmy might bring some wonderful ideas or thoughtful contributions to whatever it is we are doing.

This dynamic can be found in our friendships as well. Some of us have had very dear friends who, at some point, did something that hurt us deeply. They did that one thing that was unforgivable and now we are no longer friends. Every time we think of them, we think of that violation of our trust and may even think of them as terrible people. Those individuals become the one thing they did to us.

But what about all of the wonderful things they did with and for us during our friendship? Are they also those things? Or are they just the one thing they did that hurt us? Even if that one thing they did happened many years ago, we still think of them in the same way, as if they have not changed at all over the years. Have you ever done anything harmful to a friend or made a mistake that hurt him or her? Does that one action define who you are? Have you changed since then? Have you learned how to be a better friend over time?

If we look at our own experiences and growth over time, we may find the person we don't like is also capable of being a loving and kind person at times. In fact, we will notice that we all do hurtful things, and we all do kind things.

It's funny when someone we don't like tells a lie; we then label him a liar and that's what he becomes. We tell people he is a liar. Have we ever lied? Is that who we are? If that is the case, I think it's safe to say that we are all liars. We have all also told the truth. Is that who we are? Are we honest people or liars? I would submit that we are neither, but we do both. There is no one label that can define the totality of who and what we are. It is important to remember this in our interactions with others and to not define them with a quick and overgeneralized label.

Welcome to the Real World

Essentially, the main cause of our unhappiness is a fundamental misperception of ourselves and the world around us. Despite all evidence to the contrary, our mind presents us with a vision of the world that ultimately has little basis in reality. Trying to cultivate genuine happiness under these circumstances is like planting apple seeds and hoping to grow oranges. If we want to truly live a meaningful life and cultivate inner peace and genuine happiness, we need to understand the true sources of peace and happiness and develop their conditions in the real world.

A common belief is that we live in a world in which, if we exercise and eat right, we will be healthy and live long; if we maintain our cars, they won't break down; if we cultivate healthy relationships, they will last long; and if we work hard and get the right job, we will have job security.

But in the real world, life is messy. No matter how healthy our food is or how much we exercise, we can become ill, develop a fatal disease, or die in an accident. Cars can break down, even if they are well maintained. Relationships come and go and change over time, and so do jobs.

This misperception of our world becomes a significant problem because it causes us to be ill prepared for the realities of life when they occur. Even though we see advertisements for cancer centers, marriage and family counselors, or unemployment offices, and can find an auto repair shop on any number of street corners, we somehow don't think they should be a part of our life. As a result, we often feel as if we are victims or that life is unfair when such things happen to us. However, if we understand that these things are part of the nature of life, we are much better able to respond to the challenges and opportunities that are presented.

This is an extremely critical point. We need to understand the rules of this game called life if we want to play successfully. The world we live in has hospitals because people get injured and have illnesses. The world has therapists and counselors because people struggle to get along with each other and interact in the world. There are auto repair shops because cars break down, plumbers because toilets back up, cemeteries because people die, and emergency relief because natural disasters happen. The world we live in has crime, poverty, injustice, and economic fluctuations. This is simply the nature of things.

Despite knowing this, all too often our mind tells us that we should not need a therapist, become ill or injured, have a car break down, be a victim of crime, or die at a young age. It's as if the rules of life don't apply to us. We see these things happen to other people all the time, yet we firmly believe they should not happen to us or to our loved ones. Consequently, when something does happen, we can feel that life is unfair and ask, "Why me?" But, why not? Why should we be exempt from the rules that apply to everyone else? This is the ground from which suffering grows—the belief that things should be different from the way they are.

To be clear, in this context "suffering" refers to mental and emotional pain, not physical pain. While we have very little control over physical pain, we have incredible opportunities to reduce and even eliminate suffering. If we take a moment to examine an instance of mental and emotional suffering in our life, we will inevitably find that at its source was a desire for things to be different from what they were. The suffering comes from our inability to accept what is happening, rather than from the actual event. Our belief that harmful or unpleasant events should not happen to us fuels our inability to accept the reality of the situation. This is an empowering realization, but the delusion that opposes it is extremely difficult to break through.

Learning to accept and live in reality is the key to cultivating the life we want to live. It is learning to plant orange seeds if we expect oranges to grow. Acceptance is the foundation for developing inner peace, stability, strength, and wisdom. Acceptance doesn't mean that we necessarily like what is happening; it means we can see the situation clearly, we have stopped resisting it, and we are ready to do what we can to start improving it. Until we are able to accept and understand something, it is difficult to improve it or grow from it. The sooner we can do this, the less suffering we will experience because the suffering is tied to the resistance to what's happening much more than it is tied to the actual event. It is also, as I have been illustrating, directly related to our perspective and our emotional and mental state when the event occurs.

A helpful bit of wisdom found in many therapeutic settings is "Don't 'should' on yourself and don't 'should' on others." How many times do we think, *I should have done this*, or *They should have done that*? This is an excellent way to create mental rumination and emotional agitation. It is also usually based entirely in delusion. Whenever we use "should have," "shouldn't have," or better yet, "if only," when discussing a past event, it is speculation and fiction. As soon as we start using those words, we are watering the seeds of our dissatisfaction and unhappiness.

In truth, we don't know what would have happened—because it never did. We can make up wonderful stories of how incredible things would have turned out if only they were different. However, this wonderful turn of events exists only in our mind. Rather than accepting and engaging with what actually happened, we spend an enormous amount of time dwelling on the unreal possibilities of what might have been.

Let me illustrate this with some events from my own life. In 2013, I learned that one of my teachers was leading a two-month retreat in Thailand covering the specific training I was most focused on developing in my life. I was thrilled and set about creating the conditions and acquiring the resources to be able to attend. A dear friend of mine then asked me if I would be willing to lead a spiritual pilgrimage around Mount Kailash in Tibet. The catch was that it was scheduled during the same time as the retreat, so I would have to choose one or the other. I took some time to reflect and calculated that my teacher would be offering additional retreats in the future, but that I may never get another opportunity to travel to Tibet on such a sacred journey. So I let go of the retreat and chose to prepare and train for the spiritual, mental, and physical demands of the trek around Mount Kailash.

Fortunately, I had just moved to Carbondale, Colorado, which is surrounded by 14,000-foot peaks. To get into shape and adjust to the altitude I would experience on Mount Kailash, I would go on daily hikes above 12,000 feet. Initially, this was quite arduous and it felt as if my lungs would explode on even the shortest of hikes. However, as things do when we practice, it got easier, and I began to deeply enjoy my time in the mountains.

A couple of days before the pilgrimage trip, I took one last hike, this time with my significant other, Laura. It was incredibly beautiful. We saw gorgeous lakes, hopped across scree fields, and enjoyed the vast expanses of the Rocky Mountains. When we were at the end of the trail, near the parking lot, I was happy, playful, and turned to say something to Laura. As I did so, my foot went into a hole and my left knee contorted, tearing my cartilage and damaging my tibia plateau. It was physically painful.

So I'm in a situation where my knee is damaged and I will not be able to go to Tibet, nor will I be attending the retreat in Thailand. The most common thing people said to me was that they were so sorry and that I must be very disappointed. I'm fortunate to have so many wonderful friends who care deeply about me, and I was grateful for their concern. But was there actually something to be disappointed about?

This is where my mind can easily spin a tale about how I missed an amazing, once-in-a-lifetime spiritual journey around Mount Kailash. However, is that true? Since I didn't go on the journey, I actually have no idea what would have happened. While my mind tells me about the wonders I missed, it does not even consider that had I been able to go, I could have been robbed, or that I could have been severely injured trekking, or that I may have fallen off a cliff and died. In fact, one of the participants did get injured and was unable to finish the pilgrimage.

Likewise, my mind could quickly return to second-guessing my decision about the retreat. If only I had picked the retreat instead. Again, the mind provides so much fodder for storytelling, rumination, and effectively torturing oneself about things that never happened. As with the trip to Tibet, I never did go on that retreat and have absolutely no idea what would've happened.

Fortunately, because of the kindness and wisdom of my teachers and the training they had imparted upon me over the years, my mind did not go to any of those scenarios. Instead, it engaged in the present moment assessing what was actually happening and bringing perspective to it. Immediately, I had gratitude that I was injured so close to the car. Laura and I were able to make it there easily and she was able to drive me home. I had insurance and was able to get in to see a doctor quickly. Laura took great care of me, and I was able to rehabilitate my leg and catch up on my own studies and personal practice.

Because of this, I was not disappointed for myself at all. I was disappointed that I was unable to fulfill my commitment to the wonderful group of people who had hoped to share the pilgrimage with me. It was tough to call my dear friend and let her know that I was not able to join them. But other than that, I was deeply grateful for my incredible good fortune. I did not get injured way up in the mountains; it happened near the car. There were many times in my life when I did not have insurance, and this time I did. Laura was with me and able to care for me. This actually gave us a lot of time together, and she is now my wife. I was able to slow down and catch up on my own restorative practices. My knee was able to heal, and I can enjoy hiking again.

I tell this story to demonstrate that the events in our lives are not in and of themselves all good or all bad, all terrible or all wonderful. How we perceive them is a reflection of our own subjective experience of them, our beliefs, and the stories our mind creates around them. What matters most is not what happens; it is how we perceive and respond to what happens. The quicker we are able to accept reality and deal with things as they are, instead of how we want them to be or think they should be, the easier it is to make healthy decisions and improve the situation and the quality of our life.

A Troubled Life Transformed

As I mentioned earlier, I was a very troubled young man. I tried to solve my problems and emotional pain with alcohol and other drugs. Obviously, this did not prove to be effective; instead, it created substantially more pain and suffering.

I became a father when my daughter was born just a few hours after my twentieth birthday. My father had died when I was just six years old, and I never really knew him. This created an empty hole in my life and a sense of loss that I carried with me. Becoming a father was important to me, and I took it seriously. I did not want my daughter to be without a father as I had been. Yet, in spite of this, primarily because of my use of alcohol and other drugs, I was a terrible father and an emotionally abusive partner. As a result of my behavior, my partner left me, taking with her our daughter and the two boys whom I had tried to care for as a stepfather. She hid the children from me for eight years. Was that a terrible situation? I was a miserable wreck of a young man, and I had lost all contact with my daughter.

Over the course of the next two years, from the time I lost her into the early phase of my recovery, I would frequently whine and complain about the unfairness of it all to anyone who would listen. One day an old wise man told me, "I don't know if you'll ever get your daughter back, but if she ever comes looking for you, be someone worth finding." That was an incredible bit of wisdom.

I had no idea if I would ever see my daughter again, nor if I had any power over the situation. However, I did have power over my own actions and whether or not I would become someone worth finding. Whether I saw my daughter again or not, I could make my life meaningful. My emotional suffering eventually became great enough to provoke the realization that would transform my life.

That was August of 1984, just a few weeks before my twenty-second birthday. Since that time, I have not taken any alcohol or other mind-altering substances and have dedicated myself to working for the benefit of others and becoming "someone worth finding."

As fate would have it, I did get the precious opportunity to meet my daughter again, by far one of the most incredible and treasured experiences of my life to date. It was March 24, 1991, and my daughter was now eight-and-a-half years old. I had not seen her since she was ten months. I was nervous and excited. I did not know how she would respond to me. She had no knowledge of me and had been living in very difficult circumstances.

Would she be afraid of me? Would she be upset with me? Would she want a hug? Those questions and thoughts were running through my mind as I neared her home. I got out of the car, trembling but moving quickly. I was in such a hurry to see her, nothing was going to stop me from getting to that door!

Then the door opened, and I saw my long-lost daughter. There she stood, in her best dress, waiting to meet her father. My heart melted, and she immediately ran up and hugged me tightly. We had found each other—I had become someone worth finding.

I was given the incredible gift of a second chance to raise my daughter. I also had the unexpected pleasure of meeting her younger half-sister, who became a second daughter to me. My daughter is now an amazing young woman, married to a wonderful man and raising two kids of her own, giving me the joy of being a grandparent. As I write this, her half-sister has just become engaged and is flourishing in her life as well.

So, was losing my daughter a terrible thing? Or was it an opportunity to look deeply at the root of my suffering? What if her mother had never left me? Would I have had such a transformative life?

Often, when we look back at the painful and difficult events of our lives, we find they were the times of our greatest personal growth. The challenges of our lives provide us the opportunity to develop our highest potentials. Of course, this is not always the way we see it at the time or the way we choose to respond to our difficulties. In the early part of my life, I chose to be a victim, believing every story my mind presented and every feeling as fact. I had no training or understanding of how deceptive the mind can be or the transient nature of feelings. It took a lot of suffering for me to become willing to be teachable and try something new.

Although I'm far from perfect and had to learn most of these lessons the hard way, most of the time I'm able to engage in the moments of my life with acceptance and clarity. I have learned how to experience them as they actually are and without all of the storytelling and labeling my mind would like to present. That alone has eliminated an incredible amount of needless mental and emotional suffering in my life.

Beware of Comparisons

Another common way in which we can create dissatisfaction through misperception is by comparing our lives, and how we feel internally, with how others appear externally. When we look at the world, it is easy to find people who seem to have lives that are far better than ours, free of struggles. Such people who don't seem to suffer from insecurities, fears, depression, or other hardships. But when we compare the way we feel on the inside with how others appear on the outside, it is a recipe for dissatisfaction.

All of us have struggles, but most of us rarely show them to the outside world. Most people do not post their sadness on Facebook or other social media platforms; they post their vacations and other good times. If we were to evaluate the lives of people by the photos in their albums and on their mantels at home, we would believe that they live a wondrous life filled with love and joy, free of sadness, loss, and frustration. But people do not print and enlarge the photos that expose their difficult times. Whether they have lots of wealth and resources, many friends, or a job that commands respect, they still know sadness, disappointment, fear, and loss. As we look at others who seem to have their lives together and be free of suffering, they may well be looking at us thinking the same thing.

Rein in the Mind

Through all of these examples, we can clearly see problems created by allowing our unruly mind to drag us around from one thought to another, one story to another, one rumination to another, constantly distracting us with misperceptions and taking our attention away from what is actually happening in the present moment. To cultivate genuine happiness, inner peace, and a meaningful life, it is essential to rein in the mind and train it to work for us rather than against us.

Through mindfulness training, we are able to bring our mind consciously into the moments, events, and activities of our lives without the projections, storytelling, and elaboration that takes us away from reality. When we are able to consistently bring our minds back to the true nature of life and what is actually happening, we can engage our lives in healthy and meaningful ways—regardless of whether we are experiencing a pleasurable or not so pleasurable event. Our lives, as well as the lives of others, are filled with both. Simply knowing this empowers us to accept and respond to life as it happens instead of wishing it were different.

Of course, this is easier said than done. It is a practice, and so it takes time and effort. However, in this practice it is possible to see significant gains in meaningful ways rather quickly. The alternative is to live a life that is constantly at the mercy of outer circumstances, a roller-coaster ride of temporary moments of wide-ranging emotions, from suffering to joy, without any sense of real stability or lasting inner peace.

Three Misperceptions: Permanence, Happiness, and Identity

We have discussed many different ways our mind gets us in trouble by misperceiving the world around us. There are three primary misperceptions we hold about ourselves and the world around us. Understanding these, and the truth behind them, helps us see and experience the world more clearly and prevents us from creating more distress in our lives.

Permanence

The first misperception is that things are permanent. In reality, things in the phenomenological world that we experience are impermanent. Everything is changing all the time, including us. Everything that comes together eventually comes apart. While you maintain many of the same qualities, you are not the same person you were a year ago or even yesterday. This is also true of everyone else and everything else. Even though we may understand this intellectually, we constantly get into trouble by viewing things as permanent when they are not. We can spend a lot of time and energy acting as if inherently impermanent things are permanent and experience much hardship as result.

There are many blatant, as well as subtle ways we struggle when we forget the nature of things is impermanence and change. The most obvious example—one that affects us all directly—is death. There are two indisputable facts about death: Death is certain, and time of death is uncertain. Our mind may tell us that we are going to live for many years and to expect our friends and family will as well. We can look at odds and statistics, comforting ourselves with the idea that most people generally live a certain number of years.

However, in truth, we have no idea how long any of us will live. We all know people who have died very young, very old, suddenly, or quite slowly. Even with this knowledge, we don't think that we or our friends and family should come to untimely deaths. When it does happen, it can create an enormous amount of grief. Even a timely death after a long, well-lived life can create suffering as we struggle with the reality of death and loss. While there is a normal, healthy, grieving process that expresses our sadness for the loss of a loved one, a greater degree of grief and distress often arises from our resistance to the death.

Remembering that death is certain and time of death is uncertain for all of us, rather than having morbid thoughts about it, empowers us to participate fully in the life we do have. It reminds us that this day is truly precious and will never come again. It reminds us to focus on what is truly important in our lives while we still have the time. It reminds us to not carry petty resentments, harbor ill will, go to sleep angry with our loved ones, or put off developing our values until later. It reminds us to make every day meaningful and that each day is an opportunity to grow.

Native Americans have a wonderful saying: "Today is a good day to die." This is to say that their life has been full and meaningful, and they have no regrets. Their loved ones know that they are loved, and they have lived a life they feel good about. I believe setting the motivation to make every day a good day to die would be a most fulfilling way to live. How many times have we said, "I can't wait for this day to end"? We might want to rethink that, as each day in our life will never come again and brings us closer to our inevitable death. We don't have control over how many days we have in our life, but we do have control over how much life we have in our days.

There are many subtle ways in which change also creates struggles in our lives. We often think our job should not change, and it does. We think our relationship should not change, but it will. We may become very attached to our plan for the day, a vacation, or a project, and when things change—such as someone not showing up, a delayed flight, or some other unforeseen circumstance—we struggle because we had a plan and it *should* have gone that way. The quicker we can adjust to new circumstances and simply change our plan, the easier and more enjoyable our experience will be.

I live in a small town in the mountains and, inevitably, I will talk to some old-timer who will woefully tell me how the town has changed, reflecting on how wonderful it used to be. How many times do we do this in our own lives, reflecting on how good things used to be and how they should not have changed? If we can remember that life is fluid and everything changes all the time, then we are able to adapt and adjust our plans and our responses to whatever arises. We can engage in every day with an awareness of its preciousness instead of taking it for granted.

Searching for Happiness

The second misperception we hold about ourselves and our world is that life can provide us with lasting happiness. It is a mark of existence that the nature of the world we live in is unsatisfactory. As I've detailed, the external circumstances of our life cannot provide lasting happiness. At best, they can bring us temporary satisfaction or pleasure. There is nothing wrong with temporary pleasures and creating a comfortable and conducive lifestyle; the point is to understand the pleasures we receive from people, events, and things in our lives are always limited. If we don't realize this, we fall victim to the pervasive delusion that despite our experience, if we could just line up the outer circumstances in our life the way we would like, we would find lasting and deep happiness.

Because of this delusion, many of us spend our whole lives "looking for happiness in all the wrong places." Since I've already discussed this at length, there is no need to expand on it further now, except to point out once again that this is one of the three primary sources of our mental and emotional suffering. As long as we have an unrealistic expectation that our outer circumstances can provide lasting happiness, genuine happiness will be elusive.

Identity—Who Are We, Really?

The third misperception we hold is a misperception of self. This mark of existence is usually called "non-self." While there can be extensive philosophical and spiritual discussions about the technical meaning of non-self, I will present some of the universal ways we experience self-misperceptions that can create suffering in our lives.

It is natural we have a rather strong and concrete perception of ourselves that we carry with us throughout our days. We believe fairly confidently that we are the same person today as we were yesterday. But are you the same person today as you were yesterday? Are you the same person you were five years ago? Are you the same person you were ten years ago?

As I mentioned when discussing impermanence, everything is changing all the time—including us. In every moment, our bodies are changing, we are having new experiences and we are subject to a wide range of emotional states that come and go. Every day we have the opportunity to learn new things and develop new skills, and we are capable of cultivating new habits and tendencies. In spite of this, we usually have a fairly stagnant perception of ourselves: how we view our body, our intelligence, our abilities, our personality, and our limitations. For example, we may identify ourselves as a morning person or a night person, good at languages or terrible at languages, a natural dancer or a poor dancer, funny or not funny, a good speaker or a boring speaker, shy or boisterous, and so on. While any of these qualities might be prominent in our life at a particular time, they are always changing and consciously changeable. They are not who we are.

If we identify strongly with specific qualities that manifest in our lives at any particular time, we can create a lot of distress and risk limiting our potential for growth. For much of my early life, I had extremely low self-esteem. As a youth, I could not speak clearly and needed extensive speech therapy just to be understood. I had never thought of myself as smart, or even likable. I distinctly remember the first day of school in eighth grade. I entered my math class and instantly recognized I was in the wrong place. I looked around and saw all of the smart kids and knew there must have been a mistake. I stepped outside to check the room number and my class assignment. They matched, so I entered the room again, only to step back out quite flustered. Eventually, I walked up to the teacher, handed him my schedule and explained that there had to be a mistake. He confidently stated there was no mistake and told me to take a seat. Where do you think I sat? That's right. I sat in the back of the class, convinced I did not belong and I was incapable of succeeding.

The grade I received at the end of the term was a D, and I got that mostly just for showing up. It wasn't until much later that I discovered I had been selected for that class based on my test scores, and I actually had an aptitude for math and logic. When I finally entered college, I still perceived myself as a struggling student. I expected it to be challenging, but this time I had some years of recovery in my life and a lot of support. So while I expected it would be difficult, I was up for the challenge. As things turned out, college never became difficult for me and was actually rewarding. I was on the honor roll every year, earned a scholarship and an award, and graduated magna cum laude.

This is just one example of the myriad ways we limit ourselves based on a misperception of our own abilities and talents. Worse yet, we compare ourselves to others and define ourselves based on faulty information. We have carried most of the perceptions we have about ourselves since childhood; they become ingrained, as if they were actually us.

To grow and develop new skills and abilities, it is important we challenge the old limitations about ourselves that we cling to. There is no way this once shy, shame-based, pessimistic, speech-impaired young man with low self-esteem could have ever imagined becoming a confident public speaker and educator, helping people overcome challenges and develop genuine happiness in their lives.

When I taught high school, I used to have a sign in the front of the classroom that read, "If you think you can't, you're right." That is an incredibly powerful self-fulfilling prophecy. To develop new skills and abilities, you need to be willing to try—and also to fail. There is so much in our lives that goes unexplored simply because we don't believe in the possibility of success, or because we are so afraid we don't even make an effort. This is not to say we will be successful in cultivating any ability we like, but it reminds us that we all have untapped potentials that we have yet to explore. The other sign I had in front of my class was "The only thing that separates the person you are from the person you want to be is the action you take." This has been a guiding principle in my life, and it has withstood the test of time. Every day is a new opportunity to become the person I want to be, and I am the only one who has the power to limit or cultivate my potential.

The other common way we misperceive ourselves is through our emotions. When we experience a strong emotion (such as sadness, happiness, fear, or anger) we identify ourselves with the emotion. We believe "I am sad" or "I am happy." But is that true? Are we our feelings? When we explore this a little further, we will recognize that we are not sad; we experience sadness. Sadness will come and go, and we will still be here. Likewise, happiness will come and go, and we will still be here.

Our emotions are an integral part of our lives. They provide us with valuable insights and facilitate the ability to meaningfully engage in the world around and within us. However, we are not our feelings, and feelings are not facts. Our emotions are transient, and we can go from love to hate or fear to relief in moments.

American psychologist and pioneer in the study of emotions, Paul Ekman, PhD, explains in his book, *Emotions Revealed*, that when we are triggered by an emotion, we enter into a refractory state and are unable to experience things clearly. We see everything through the lens of that particular emotion and are unable to take in and hear information about what is actually happening. If we are experiencing loneliness, we see everything through our loneliness and may even have the thought that we will always be lonely. In the midst of the emotion, we become so identified with that feeling we forget it is temporary and often make decisions under its influence that we will regret later. By cultivating mindfulness, we are able to develop the ability to experience an emotion without the need to identify with it or push it away. In the process, we give ourselves the space to respond in a healthy and intentional way.

This reminds me of a Facebook post I saw that had quite a bit of wisdom in it: "Never make a decision when you're angry, or a promise when you are happy." The actions we take can have a much longer life than our feelings do.

Chapter Seven

Cultivating the Four Immeasurable Attitudes

"As a single footstep will not make a path on the earth, so a single thought will not make a pathway in the mind. To make a deep physical path, we walk again and again. To make a deep mental path, we must think over and over the kind of thoughts we wish to dominate our lives." Henry David Thoreau

As we become more mindful in our daily lives, we will discover that we actually have more freedom and choice than we had ever imagined. Our outer circumstances will no longer feel so constrictive, nor will they dictate habitual responses that limit our ability to establish free will in our lives. By free will, I mean the ability to choose one thought over another; to stop doing things we don't feel good about; to stop giving in to habits, tendencies, and impulses we know create problems for us; to consciously initiate actions and respond rather than react to whatever happens in life in ways that are in alignment with our values. This need not be some lofty goal that seems far removed from us—our free will is in the here and now and becomes stronger with every mindful thought we have.

We have the ability to proactively set our intentions and cultivate the thoughts, as well as the mental states we would like to develop. Neuroscientific research has demonstrated that we can actually rewire our brains. Our thoughts and experiences can change both the brain's physical structure and its functional organization. As we develop new habits and thought patterns, just as if we were making a path in the forest, we are creating new neural pathways in our brain. Neurons that fire together wire together. While science now validates this concept, it has been known throughout time, clearly illuminated by philosophers such as Aristotle and found in the teachings of many cultures.

Consider this well-worn Native American parable: One evening, a wise old grandfather told his grandson about a battle that goes on inside people. He said, "My son, the battle is between two wolves that are inside us all. One is filled with anger, envy, jealousy, greed and resentment. The other is filled with love, joy, peace, kindness, and truth." The grandson thought about it for a minute and then asked his grandfather, "Which wolf wins?" The grandfather replied, "The one you feed."

This is a valuable lesson that reminds us it is extremely important to be aware of the thoughts, attitudes, and emotions we are feeding. All of our actions are preceded and initiated by mental activities, such as thoughts or emotions. Sometimes these are very subtle and happen quickly, but if you look closely you will see that they do. The words we choose, the actions we engage in, and the choices we make may often seem effortless, requiring little thought at all. We have all impulsively, quicker than we can consciously think, said things and done things we deeply regret almost instantly. The healthier our mind is, even if we cannot consciously respond, the healthier our reactions will be.

The thoughts and mental and emotional states we experience condition us. Unfortunately, we experience most of them unconsciously, outside of our awareness. The good news is that we can change our conditioning. We can develop and strengthen the mental and emotional states we find beneficial. There are specific mental states that are extremely healthy and are direct antidotes to harmful ones. They include equanimity, loving-kindness, compassion, and empathetic joy. In Buddhism, these healthy states are referred to as the four immeasurable attitudes.

Teachings on each of these beneficial attitudes can be found in many spiritual traditions and cultures. However, they are taught as a cohesive unit within the Buddhist teachings known as the *brahmavihāras*, usually translated as "the four immeasurables." While they have origins in Buddhist philosophy, the benefits of cultivating the four immeasurable attitudes are universal, not bound by any particular spiritual or religious belief. In addition to helping us cultivate a healthy and open heart, which nourishes our relationship with ourselves and others, they are also the antidotes to unhealthy attachment and aversion, hatred, ill will, jealousy, and envy—just as turning on a light dispels the darkness.

The Immeasurable Attitude of Equanimity

Equanimity is often described as a mind of calm or composure. It is a balanced state of mind that does not get caught up in extremes. It allows us to be present and stable even in difficult and challenging situations, not getting entangled in and identified with overpowering emotions.

I describe equanimity as wise acceptance. It is the ability to be wisely present with and accept whatever arises in each moment. To be wisely present means to be aware of projections, elaborations, feelings, and attachments that may be limiting our ability to accept and see what is happening clearly. Again, accepting what is happening does not mean we like it or are unwilling to change it. It means we understand that it *is* happening and that there is a reason for it. It is neither all good nor all bad, and whether it is pleasant or unpleasant, we have the opportunity to respond to and engage with it in a way that is beneficial and healthy.

Through the cultivation of equanimity, we learn to engage with equal attention and care in all of our experiences, including interactions with people we like, those we don't like, and strangers. While this may sound difficult to achieve, every day we can make progress in cultivating a mind that is balanced, clear, and does not get caught up in exaggerations. You may notice that when we are calm, it is much easier to make decisions and choices that are healthy for us. However, when we are challenged or caught up in emotions such as sadness, fear, anger, or even happiness, it can become difficult to bring that same clarity of mind to our decisions. One of the keys to cultivating equanimity is to start noticing how we exaggerate the good and bad qualities in people, events, and simple activities in our lives.

Equanimity is often confused with indifference. Equanimity does not mean or imply that we don't have preferences; it does not mean that we don't care what happens. It actually empowers us to bring a deep level of attention, care, and concern into all of our interactions and experiences, whether or not we like what is happening.

With equanimity, we are able to use the wisdom we have cultivated about how the world actually is and accept what is happening without letting our projections get in the way. This allows us to make healthy decisions we will feel good about over time, instead of impulsive reactions we will regret. So we can see there is a preference—a preference to not let our mind and emotions interfere with our free will. There is a preference to make healthy decisions and to engage in life in ways that are in alignment with our values.

Equanimity is the antidote to unhealthy attachment and aversion. As discussed in the chapter on happiness, so much of the time our unhealthy attachments are actually the source of our mental and emotional suffering. Aversion is just another form of attachment; it is a state of being attached to something not happening in our lives. We create an incredible amount of unnecessary suffering by trying to resist and avoid the natural and legitimate pain that comes with life.

As Thomas Merton, the renowned contemplative, author, and Trappist monk, puts it so clearly, "The one who does most to avoid suffering is, in the end, the one who suffers most." Eminent psychologist Carl Jung stated that "neurosis is always a substitute for legitimate suffering."

The sooner we are able to deal with the difficult or unpleasant challenges that arise in our life, the less suffering we will have. Trying to avoid something automatically creates stress. Often, difficulties we put off grow and become much bigger problems. This is not to say we should look for challenges. Trust me, there will be enough that come our way on their own. Nor does it mean we should not try to avoid unnecessary difficulties. Again, equanimity does not exclude preferences or wise choices. Common analogies include enduring the pain of a root canal to eliminate nerve pain and further infection, and ending an unhealthy relationship instead of remaining in it to avoid the emotional pain a breakup will bring.

In training to cultivate equanimity, it is common to start with our relationships with others. In general, we put people into one of three categories: people we like, people we dislike, and people we are rather neutral about, such as strangers or those we don't know well. The goal of equanimity is to recognize the value in all beings, whether we like them or not, and treat them with an equal level of concern and attention.

Why do we like some people and dislike others? Take a moment to call to mind some of the people you enjoy being around. What makes them so enjoyable? Is it that they are kind to you? Do they share the same perspectives and values that you do? Are they funny?

Now take a moment to call to mind people you don't like. Why don't you like them? Are they mean? Are they inconsiderate? Are their values and perspectives different from yours? Do you think they wake up every day and want to be disliked? Are they inherently bad people?

When we take a little time to explore these questions, it is not unusual to find that we like people who think the same way we do. We like people who are nice to us. We like people who have interests, values, and beliefs that are similar to ours. Conversely, we tend to dislike people who do not share our views and values, people who don't treat us kindly, and people who are not enjoyable to be around.

There is one common factor in all the people we like and don't like: It is us. We tend to judge all others based on our values and belief systems. We start labeling people—as funny, attractive, mean, stupid, brilliant, valuable, boring, etc.—based on our own values and how we think people should be, not taking into account that their values make sense to them based upon the way they were raised and their life experiences. It is an interesting phenomenon in that we want to be treated equally yet are unable to treat others equally. We have a fondness for our friends even when they display poor judgment, possibly hurting others. We have animosity toward those we dislike even when they are doing something kind. There are others whom we don't care about one way or the other, usually because we don't know them or have not had much experience with them.

Should everyone be treated equally? Is everyone valuable? Can people change? Have you changed? Have your values changed? Have your belief systems changed? Have you done things that hurt people? Have you done things that have helped people? Have you made mistakes that you regret? Do you think others have? As we reflect on these questions and how we label and judge others, we may find the people we are attracted to are far from perfect, and the people we don't like are not inherently flawed.

In trainings on developing equanimity and compassion, participants are commonly taught to bring to mind these simple truths: Everyone is trying to find happiness and everyone is trying to avoid suffering. In this way, we are all equal.

Just like you, everyone is trying to be happy.

Just like you, everyone is trying to avoid suffering.

Just like you, everyone has known sadness and despair.

Just like you, everyone is trying to get their needs met.

Just like you, everyone is learning how to live.

If we understand all people are trying to find their way, learning how to live, and generally doing the best they can with what they have, it helps us recognize and honor their value. This does not mean we disregard harmful things they might do. People sometimes do harmful things, including violent things. We need to be clear about this and bring wisdom and discernment into our equanimity.

In my career, I've had the opportunity to work with and counsel many individuals who have inflicted violence on others and even killed people. In all my years of experience, through thousands of sessions with people, I have never met anyone who deep down wanted to be a bad person. I've never met an addict who wanted to be an addict. I've never met an abusive partner who wanted to be abusive to his or her partner. I have met many other human beings, just like me, who were trying to find their way and feel good about who they are. Though they may exist, I have never met an abuser who did not have a history of being abused. Even the toughest gang members I've met could list a long history of physical and emotional abuse, usually beginning at a very early age.

Every year I go on a weekend retreat with 120 other men. All of them, including me, are in recovery and spent many years harming others. Many of them have spent some time in prison and, earlier in their lives were not people you would have wanted to meet in a dark alley. We come together to open our hearts, develop our spiritual path, and learn how we can be of more benefit to others. When we greet each other, we do not shake hands; we hug and say, "I love you." These men are my dear friends, and I'm honored to learn and grow with them. They have dedicated their recovery to opening their hearts, living meaningful lives, and helping others.

Are these bad men? If you had met them years ago, you might well have thought so. Are they good men? I've done an incredible number of harmful things in my life. Am I a bad man? I have spent the majority of the past thirty years helping others. Am I a good man? In truth, these men are not good or bad, and neither am I. We are just human. We all have done things we regret, and we all have done things we feel good about. However, at no point did we intentionally decide to destroy our lives or hurt others. We are all trying to find our way, and people tend to give what they have. Those who have a lot of pain, tend to give pain to others. And those who have a lot of love, tend to give love to others.

We all have the capacity to change. You may know people in your life who had always been dependable and trustworthy and then, at some point, took a turn for the worse and became untrustworthy. Likewise, my retreat friends and I share stories of redemption in which we received the support necessary to transform ourselves into kind and beneficial members of society. The point to remember is that the labels we stick on people never tell the whole story. Is anyone better than anyone else? Or did some of us have the good fortune to have more emotional support and/or more resources than others?

I used to work at a large urban high school in a low-income area. Teaching at such schools can be extremely challenging, so they tend to draw a remarkably resilient and dedicated faculty. We had to have those qualities to thrive and make a difference in the lives of our students. Those with less dedication would burn out or quit.

At my school, there was a quirky teacher; I will call Jim. A joke among staff members at the school was to ask, "What is the hardest thing in the world?" When they got the typical answer—a diamond—they would say, "No, the hardest thing in the world is ending a conversation with Jim." In fact, it was difficult to end a conversation with Jim. Every time we saw him, he had lots to share. He would even follow us into our classrooms to continue voicing his ideas and thoughts.

Of course, as overworked schoolteachers with a lot on our plates, the rest of us found it taxing to have the time and patience to listen to Jim. Many of my other colleagues and I came to see Jim as someone to avoid. Another thing we often sought to avoid was the dreaded faculty meeting. Though deep down we all recognized that it was important to have meetings, we were so busy with our work and our students that we found it difficult to give up our time. Occasionally, just as a faculty meeting would be nearing an end, the meeting leader would ask if anyone had comments, and Jim would take the opportunity to grab the microphone. The staff would let out a collective sigh of exasperation as Jim began to offer us his wisdom.

Having received teachings on equanimity, I decided to apply them to Jim. Instead of focusing on the qualities in him that I was seeking to avoid, I sought to learn about and recognize his good qualities. As it turned out, there were many.

Jim had taught at the school for fifteen years. In all that time, he had never missed a day for illness—a remarkable achievement. I had managed to do a couple of years without missing a day and thought I had really accomplished something. In that type of environment, it is not uncommon for teachers to need some mental health days in addition to normal sick days. But Jim was there every day. Not only that, he also arrived early and stayed late, offering tutoring for his students on his own time. When I reflected on what Jim was always talking about, I realized it was always about ways to engage the students.

The more I learned about Jim, the more I admired him. He was no longer someone to avoid, but someone to emulate and learn from. The only thing that prevented me from seeing this earlier was my own self-centered attachment to the things I wanted to do and aversion to sharing my time with him.

Another thing to notice as we develop equanimity is how our labels can change over time. Strangers become friends, friends become people we dislike, people we dislike become friends, some friends even become strangers. While the labels change, does the essential nature of these people change? Does our essential nature change?

It is usually easy to love our family and friends. Most people, including me, revel in being a grandparent. I usually tell people that it's good work if you can get it. In most cases, there is almost nothing we wouldn't do to help our children, grandchildren, or parents. A whole industry is dedicated to making shirts and coffee cups that say "World's Greatest Mom," "World's Best Grandfather," and so on.

As you may recall from my earlier discussion, I love my daughters dearly and cherish the precious opportunity I have to be a father. I was actually in tears as I wrote that section of this book. But a fundamental question I asked myself early on in my training was: Why should I feel that depth of love only for my family? Is there any reason I should love you any less than I love my daughters?

This is a significant question for me. Everyone is somebody's daughter, son, brother, sister, mother, or father. Why is mine more important than yours? As I have reflected on this over the years, there is absolutely no reason I can find to love you any less than I love my daughters or granddaughters. I do have different roles and responsibilities regarding my family. However, I do not see how other lives are less valuable than mine or those of my family. I have yet to develop the capability to love you as much as I love my daughters and granddaughters, but I aspire to. And in doing so, I have been able to let go of many resentments and judgments, and start seeing the value in nearly everyone I meet.

For most of us it is much easier to see the value in others when we are able to remember how much they benefit us. It is easy to forget that everything we have, know, and are able to do is because of others. As Ralph Waldo Emerson expressed: "Cultivate the habit of being grateful for every good thing that comes to you, and to give thanks continuously. And because all things have contributed to your advancement, you should include all things in your gratitude."

Take a moment to reflect on something as simple as eating a piece of toast in the morning. How many people, as well as causes and conditions, do you think were involved in producing that piece of toast? How many people were involved in the farming process? How many people were involved in educating the farmers so they would have the technical skills required to cultivate the soil? Where did this education come from? How many machines were involved in tilling the soil and harvesting the wheat? Just reflecting on one tractor, how many people were involved in the production of it? To have tractors, the development of the combustion engine was necessary. How many people were involved in the development and production of motorized vehicles? How many people were involved in forming the metals that became the tractor? What about the rubber on the tires? How many people were involved in learning how to tap trees for rubber and transform it into tires?

We haven't even gotten to the processing of the wheat or the bakery yet. What about the ovens that the bread was baked in? How many people were involved in creating those ovens? How many people work at the bakery? How many people were involved in building the bakery? How many were involved in harvesting the lumber to build the bakery? What about the lawyers, marketing department, and accountants for the bakery? How many people were involved in paying for and constructing the roads the bread was transported on? How many people are involved in creating the trucks that transported the bread? How many people were involved in the creation of the store where you bought the bread?

As you can see, I could go on endlessly, and this is only for a piece of bread. Our education, our clothing, our entertainment, our employment—quite literally everything we have and enjoy—is because of others. Even our annoying or difficult customer or client is the reason we have a job.

Our mind wants to separate the world into "me and mine" and "you and yours." As soon as we do this, in addition to seeing the world inaccurately, we create a tension between us and more than seven billion others. We will not find any lasting inner peace in attending only to the needs of "me and mine." Inner peace is present, however, in "we and ours."

Once again, when we understand the world more accurately, including that we are not as independent as we think, we can reduce a lot of unnecessary stress in our lives. The world we live in is an interdependent place, and it is to our benefit that others are healthy, happy, and have opportunity. When others have these things, they are not resorting to breaking into cars, hurting people, or committing other crimes. Even the people with whom we have the most difficulty may have truly helped us.

Just as our challenges have helped us to develop our inner strength, the difficult people in our lives (usually as a result of their own suffering) have helped us to discover our own untapped resources. Realizing this allows us to forgive. When we forgive others, we give ourselves permission to let go of our own suffering. This is a powerfully transformative reflection. As I mentioned before, it is very easy to be attached to our past resentments and challenges. We often wear them like merit badges and dredge up how we were harmed by others and by circumstances. This can instantly bring up anger, pain, self-righteousness, or simply keep the wound fresh so that it has no opportunity to heal. Instead, we can choose to reflect on how those people and events taught us valuable lessons or presented us with opportunities to develop ourselves. I suggest you reflect upon some of the difficult people and events from your past and see if you can find ways in which they have benefited you. See if you can update the story you've told yourself about what happened. Maybe the new story can be a little more comprehensive and beneficial than the old one.

Equanimity is not limited to our relationships with others; it is a profoundly wise acceptance of things as they are. It can be applied to all of the events, activities, and internal and external circumstances of our lives. It provides us access to a clear and calm mind that does not get caught up in exaggerations and storytelling. The immeasurable attitude of equanimity allows us to enjoy a delicious meal without the thought that this is the best meal ever. It also allows us to be grateful to have a meal that we don't find delicious, recognizing that so many people have no food. When difficulties or challenges arise, the immeasurable attitude of equanimity empowers us to wisely accept and rise to them. It is not indifferent; it has a preference—a preference that remains grounded in reality and provides an opportunity for us to make healthy choices.

The Immeasurable Attitude of Loving-Kindness

The immeasurable attitude of loving-kindness is the deep and sincere wish for ourselves and all others to be happy. It is not an attached love or kindness focused only on people we like or on those who are kind to us. It is embedded in our understanding that we are connected to all others. We become able to see all others as if they were dear old friends, and we want the very best for them. When our dear old friends make mistakes or do something we dislike, we are able to forgive them and maintain our friendship.

When we cultivate loving kindness, we are cultivating the direct antidote to the mental and emotional states of anger and hatred. As Martin Luther King Jr. expressed, "Hatred paralyzes life; love releases it. Hatred confuses life; love harmonizes it. Hatred darkens life; love illuminates it." We cannot have love and hate for the same thing at the same time. Although love can quickly turn to hate and hate into love, they cannot exist simultaneously in the same moment for the same object. As I discussed at the beginning of this chapter, what you water grows. Wouldn't it be better to water the flowers of love and kindness instead of the weeds of anger and hatred?

In this way, developing the immeasurable attitude of loving-kindness begins with oneself. Frequently, loving-kindness can be even more difficult to practice with ourselves than with others. We can be very hard on ourselves and, sometimes, we do not feel worthy of love. I have known this feeling well in my own life, and it took me many years to learn I was just as valuable and deserving of love as anyone else. This is among the areas where the previous reflections on equanimity prove helpful and healthy, bringing to mind that all of us are valuable and are doing the best we can with what we have. None of us woke up one day and consciously decided from the depth of our heart to make mistakes and screw up our lives. Whatever we did at any given moment was ultimately the best we could do in that moment.

As I described earlier, thoughts that start with "should have" and "if only" in regard to past events are always fiction and rarely beneficial. Even when we've made mistakes and done things we regret, based on the situation and our physical, emotional, and mental states (such as fear, insecurity, or distraction) we did the best we could at that moment. We did not intentionally decide to make a mistake. This is an important truth to understand so that we can learn to forgive ourselves and let go of false perceptions that keep us stuck and prevent us from growing. With wise acceptance, we can understand and learn from our mistakes. Our mistakes provide nutrients for the soil from which we grow our wisdom and character.

Just like everyone else, we are a work in progress. Our progress increases with healthy states of mind such as love and kindness, and is halted by guilt and shame. There's nothing beneficial about beating ourselves up and thinking that somehow we are less valuable than anyone else. This does not serve us—or anyone else. The best thing we can do to correct a regret is to learn from it. The best way to make amends is to develop the wisdom and ability to change our behavior. This does not mean we are not accountable for our behaviors and mistakes. It means we are truly accountable for them and willing to make the effort to do something about them.

Whenever we experience feelings of unworthiness or low self-esteem, it is helpful to develop the habit of challenging these feelings, just as we would any other unsubstantiated accusation. Are we the regrettable things we've done? Or are we the kind and wonderful things we've done? Do we have the potential to grow? Have we grown in the past? I imagine if you were to reflect on the whole of your life you would realize that for the vast majority of it you were not doing anything harmful or regrettable. I am certain you would recognize that during most of your waking hours you were not hurting anyone, and your beneficial and helpful activities far outnumbered any harmful ones. Ultimately, you would discover that most of your days were filled with actions that were productive and helpful to yourself and others.

In spite of this, we let that one thing we regret overpower all the good we do. It becomes the primary focus of our mental and emotional states and prevents us from seeing clearly. I've been on retreats with wonderful people who have devoted their lives to cultivating compassion and kindness, yet beat up themselves when they occasionally lose their temper. In all of the amazing teachings about unconditional love, we can become inspired and strive to be that perfect, unconditionally loving person. But when we fail to be perfect, we can become hard on ourselves and fail to extend that unconditional love to ourselves.

It is important to remember that this is all a process, and just the effort to improve, whether or not we are successful at any given moment, improves us. Saint Francis of Assisi described this dynamic as follows: "You learn to speak by speaking, to study by studying, to run by running, to work by working; and just so, you learn to love by loving."

We need to start where we are and begin our journey anew every day. We need to wisely accept our mistakes as well as our achievements, our setbacks as well as our progress. To cultivate our highest potentials, we need to recognize that we have them. It is not the achievement of any of our lofty goals, but the effort and lessons we learn in achieving them that shape our lives. Where we are at any given moment is not nearly as important as how far we've come and where we are going.

We all have the capacity to cultivate the immeasurable attitude of loving-kindness—a heartfelt desire for ourselves and others to be well and genuinely happy. The traditional method is to start with ourselves. We then extend it to our friends and loved ones, and finally to strangers and those we don't like or with whom we have difficulties. In this way, beginning with ourselves, we cultivate loving-kindness for us and for all other beings.

There are many books and teachings available on methods for developing loving-kindness. The method I was trained in and have found quite valuable involves meditating on these four aspirations:

> May I be filled with loving-kindness.
> May I be peaceful and at ease.
> May I be healthy and well.
> May I be genuinely happy.

Another common set of aspirations used in developing loving-kindness is:

> May I be free from hatred.
> May I be free from anxiety.
> May I be free from illness.
> May I be well and happy.

On the surface, this may seem like a selfish practice. If we have the proper motivation, the profound impact of this practice is anything but selfish. It is ideal if we do loving-kindness practice with the motivation to develop our own highest potentials so that we can improve our interactions with others and the world at large. Essentially, we develop loving-kindness so that we have more of it to share.

As we become filled with loving-kindness, we become free of hatred. By becoming peaceful and at ease, we are freed from anxiety. By becoming healthy and well, we are freed from illness. The practice is to meditate on these four thoughts for ourselves and others and then to bring the attitude of loving-kindness into all of our daily activities. As we encounter people, including those we find difficult or challenging, we can silently wish them to be well and happy.

LOVING-KINDNESS MEDITATION

Gently bring your awareness to the sensations of the breath as it enters and exits your body. Each breath is a new moment. Be aware of this moment. Let the breath be natural. Don't worry if it's deep or shallow. Simply allow yourself to breathe.

Let each inhale be an invitation to relax, an opportunity to release any tension, worries, or concerns. Let them leave your body with the breath on your exhale. Allow yourself to be relaxed and calm, simply breathing and relaxing.

Now take a moment to give yourself permission to let go of all worries, concerns, and time constraints. Give permission to nourish yourself, to allow yourself to breathe, to cultivate love and kindness in your life, and to spread it to others. Give yourself permission to be here now, and cultivate loving-kindness.

Now cultivate the thought: *May I be filled with loving-kindness.* Here you can visualize your heart emanating a radiant warmth of love filling your whole body. It fills you with love and you feel complete acceptance, safe, and cared for. Take a little time to let this fill your whole being—feeling loved, completely accepted, cared for, and safe.

Now cultivate the thought: *May I be peaceful and at ease.* Just let your body and mind relax. As you breathe out, let go of any worries, anxieties, or fears. See yourself peaceful, relaxed, and at ease.

Now cultivate the thought: *May I be healthy and well.* Take some time to see yourself in optimal health. With each inhale you can visualize a radiant healing light going to any part of your body that may have an injury or illness. When you exhale, see that malady exit your body. See yourself becoming healthier with each breath. *May I be well.*

Now cultivate the thought: *May I be happy. May I be genuinely happy.* Here it's a good idea to put a smile on your face and call to mind a time in your life when you were filled with joy, happiness, and contentment. Bring that to mind, and let it permeate your whole body. See yourself filled with genuine happiness, well-being, and contentment.

Having cultivated these qualities within yourself, turn your mind to others. Call to mind people you care for, someone who is going through a challenging time, someone who might be in a hospital or someone who is just struggling. Bring them present as clearly as possible in front of you. Then cultivate the thought: *May they be filled with loving-kindness.* See them receiving this love and having it emanate through their whole body, just as it did yours. See them feeling accepted and cared for.

Now cultivate the thought: *May they be peaceful and at ease.* See them relaxing and letting their worries drift away.

Now cultivate the thought: *May they be well. May they be healthy.* See any physical pain easing from them. See them getting healthier.

Then cultivate the thought: *May they be happy. May they be genuinely happy.* See a smile coming to their faces. See them content. See them happy.

Next, take a little time to call to mind people you have neutral feelings about, who you don't know very well. It could be the person you pass on the way to work or a cashier at the store, possibly someone on a bus or someone you know just a little bit. Call to mind one person or several people like this.

Call them to mind and think, *They, just like me, want happiness. Just like me, they have worries, concerns, and problems. And just like me, they deserve some inner peace, love, and acceptance.* All beings want happiness and all beings want to avoid suffering. In this way, we are all equal.

With this in mind, cultivate the thought: *May they be filled with loving-kindness.* See them receiving this love just as you did. See it permeate through their whole body, making them feel accepted, cared for, and loved.

May they be peaceful and at ease. See their worries drifting away. See them peaceful and at ease.

May they be well. May they be healthy. Wish them well from your heart. See them becoming vibrant, healthy, and well.

May they be happy. May they be genuinely happy. See them smiling, happy, and content.

Now take a little time to call to mind people with whom you have difficulty, someone you have struggled to be around, or maybe someone associated with a problem you are having. Remember, just like you, they want happiness, they want to avoid suffering, and they have worries, trials and tribulations, concerns, and fears. They, too, deserve happiness.

With these people in mind, cultivate the thought: *May they be filled with loving-kindness.* See them feeling cared for, accepted, and filled with love.

May they be peaceful and at ease. See all of their struggles drifting away. See them letting go of their anxieties and fears.

May they be healthy and well. See them becoming vibrant, healthy, and well.

May they be happy, genuinely happy. See them being happy and having a sense of well-being and contentment.

Now visualize yourself with everyone you have included in this meditation and cultivate the thought: *May we be filled with loving-*

kindness. Allow that love to permeate your whole being as well as the others. See yourself and everyone else filled with love, acceptance, and kindness.

The Immeasurable Attitude of Compassion

The immeasurable attitude of compassion is complementary to that of loving-kindness. They are like two sides of the same coin. The expression of loving-kindness is the wish for ourselves and others to be truly happy, and compassion is the deep desire for ourselves and others to be free from suffering. According to His Holiness the 14th Dalai Lama, "Only the development of compassion and understanding for others can bring us to tranquility and happiness we all seek." Compassion is an incredibly powerful force that motivates us to address and confront the true sources of suffering in the lives of others as well as in our own life. It is the direct antidote to the harmful mental states of cruelty and ill will.

Compassion is often misunderstood and therefore rarely fully developed in our lives. Some people have the idea that if they are compassionate they will feel sad all the time. This is a common confusion in our culture. Compassion does not lead to sadness. It is when we recognize the sadness and suffering of ourselves or others that compassion arises. It is the result of sadness and suffering, not the cause. Out of compassion we can find the strength and wisdom to respond to life's challenges in healthy and productive ways.

Compassion also gets confused with empathy. Empathy is a vital quality to develop and is the foundation from which we cultivate compassion. However, it is not the same as compassion. With empathy, we are able to relate to, understand, and, to some degree, experience the feelings of others. This is incredibly important in enabling us to have healthy relationships. Empathy allows us to recognize and directly relate to the suffering of others, which can be a catalyst for creating compassion, the desire to remove that suffering. Unfortunately, empathy in regard to suffering does not always give rise to compassion.

Sometimes we can feel helpless as we directly experience the suffering of others, and that can lead to emotional burnout, despair, and a sense of hopelessness. This can be mischaracterized as compassion fatigue, but it is actually more accurately empathy fatigue. If we develop our empathy but do not cultivate the wisdom of compassion, which is an active source of strength for responding to and dealing with suffering, we can fall into empathy fatigue. Rather than draining us, compassion has the power to sustain, inspire, and motivate us.

Empathy can also give rise to anger, cruelty, and ill will. As I mentioned earlier, compassion is the antidote to these destructive mental and emotional states. If we are not careful, when we see or experience the suffering of others, we can become angry. As we get angry, we lose our ability to have clear judgment and our mind can turn to the source of the suffering and resort to cruelty toward others. Instead of focusing wisely on solving the suffering, a vengeful mind can arise, desiring that others suffer as well. But with compassion, we can respond to suffering with wisdom and clarity, seeking to reduce the suffering of all involved, not just in the moment but in the long term.

When I was teaching high school, one of my colleagues, in a fit of rage, started screaming at me in front of some students, accusing me of things of which I was innocent. As he was yelling at me, I could feel my body tensing and indignation rising within me. Normally, this would easily turn into justified anger, causing me to yell back and set him straight. Fortunately, because there were students around, I was conscious of my behavior in front of them. So instead of interrupting my colleague, I tried to remain calm and let him say what he needed to say. As he was yelling at me, I recognized his pain and his anger. I saw that he was extremely upset and that it was out of his suffering that he was yelling at me.

Suddenly, compassion arose instead of anger. This gave me the ability to respond rather than react. When he finished, I was able to tell him I was sorry that he was upset and then ask him if we could sit down together and talk. Instead of having a desire to inflict pain on him, I was able to show concern for him. We were able to sit down and clear up the misunderstanding. He became a dear friend of mine and one of the colleagues I truly admired.

I am fortunate the students were there. Their presence allowed me the restraint to make space for compassion to arise. Had I been immediately triggered to feel anger, the emotional power of my anger would have taken over. Rather than responding, I would have reacted—most likely with cruelty. Rather than seeing clearly what was actually happening, I could have easily demonized him for his unjustifiable and inappropriate verbal assault on me in front of students. No doubt that would have led me to react with a verbal assault of my own I would have later regretted. Not only would I have regretted my reaction, it also would not have addressed the actual cause of the suffering for either of us. Compassion is always focused on removing suffering, not creating more—even if that means enduring some suffering oneself in the present moment.

I was once in my classroom at the end of what felt like a very long day. The last of the students had finally left, and just as I was about to take a breath and relax, the phone rang. On the other end of the line was an upset parent. She immediately unleashed her anger on me and shared her low opinion of my abilities as a teacher. She had just received her child's report card and saw that he had failed.

Although I know it was only a few minutes, it seemed as if she spent an unbearable amount of time listing the many ways I was failing as a teacher. She specifically noted that I should have been in contact with her regarding her son's poor performance in my class. Now, as she was yelling at me, I was preparing my defense. In fact, I had sent notices home and tried to make contact. I had done my due diligence and had the records to prove it.

Fortunately, she was so upset and went on so long that I did not have the opportunity to inform her of the facts. As she talked, I began to realize that she was just a single mom who was worried about her son and his future. Her anger arose from her fear for him. My pointing out to her the attempts I had made to contact her would not have provided the comfort she needed at that moment. So when she finally stopped and gave me a chance to respond, I told her, "I'm very sorry. You're right. I could have done more." Technically, this was true. I was sorry, and I could have done more. But instead of putting her on the defensive, my comments allowed her to know that I had heard her concerns and allowed us to have the more important discussion of how we could work together to help her son improve.

This is not to say we don't compassionately enforce consequences for behaviors and actions that are harmful. There are good reasons to respond to malicious behavior with discipline and to have prisons, for instance. It is not showing compassion to let people harm or take advantage of us or others. That just increases suffering for everyone involved. The key is to not respond to bad behavior with cruelty and ill will, wanting people to be punished for the sake of punishment itself. The use of any discipline or punishment should be motivated by compassion, applied to improve the behavior or situation in a way that is most helpful overall.

A powerful example of how the competing forces of ill will and compassion can clash is a drunk-driving accident. According to the US Centers for Disease Control and Prevention (CDC), based on figures compiled by the National Center for Statistics and Analysis of the National Highway Traffic Safety Administration, in 2013, 10,076 people were killed in alcohol-impaired-driving crashes, accounting for nearly one-third (31 percent) of all traffic-related deaths in the United States. These are startling and tragic statistics. In fact, they are much more than statistics. The numbers represent real people: children, brothers, sisters, fathers, mothers. All of them had families, hopes, and desires— just like us.

When someone is killed by a drunk driver, especially if it's a family member or someone we know, it is natural and justified to demand accountability and justice. It is also quite natural for that to turn into a demand for retribution. It's easy to see the drunk driver as an unworthy human being, less than us, and deserving of years of suffering under a long prison sentence. We may even feel compelled to attend parole hearings and ask our friends to write letters to prevent the drunk driver from ever getting out. We may truly want the driver to suffer.

But who does this help? How does this atone for the loss of someone's life? Would we think it unjust if the drunk driver served only a two-year sentence? Would ten years be enough? Is the point of incarceration to make the driver suffer to somehow ease our pain? Could we use incarceration to alleviate suffering? To redirect a life that has made mistakes? Have you ever made some big mistakes? Have you ever driven when you are too tired or a little under the influence? How about texting while driving? Have you ever driven when you were angry? Under other circumstances, could you have been involved in an accident that took someone's life?

Personally, I have answered yes to all of these questions. Fortunately, I have never taken anyone's life, although I know there have been many instances in which it easily could have happened. Yet, when I hear about another person doing it, in the heat of the moment I can become incredulous and demand justice. For some reason, I can stop seeing that person as just another human being, who—just like me—is trying to find his or her way.

When we are angry, or under the influence of any powerful emotion, we are unable to maintain perspective and see clearly. If we recognize this and allow our emotions to subside, we will be in a much healthier position to respond with the wisdom of compassion. This empowers us to respond to the actions of the person, hold him or her accountable, and develop a consequence that balances suffering with the opportunity to improve.

One of my dear friends was responsible for the deaths of others while driving under the influence. He was young at the time and drove home drunk from a party. He does not remember the event at all, and he suffered an incredible amount of physical damage himself. He had to do extensive physical rehabilitation, and he spent time in prison and in a drug treatment program. In total, this took less than four years. Is that enough punishment? Is he a bad person who deserves more punishment?

He will live the rest of his life knowing he was responsible for those deaths. Since his release from prison, he has devoted his life to helping others and is one of the most loving and compassionate people I know. He has been a true friend to me throughout many of my ups and downs, teaching me many lessons in life. I truly admire him and all that he does for the world. Would the world be a better place if he were still in prison?

I'm not sharing this to advocate any particular position. I share these examples to illustrate that compassion gives us the opportunity to respond to and alleviate suffering more skillfully than cruelty and ill will would. Sometimes it's appropriate to lock someone up for the purpose of public safety. Sometimes it's appropriate and necessary that people suffer as a consequence of their unhealthy behaviors.

In many cases, it is only through suffering the consequences of our behaviors that we become open to changing them. This is clearly how it works in the realm of recovery. I have never met an addict who quit drinking or using other drugs because he or she thought it was a good idea. Everyone I have ever met in recovery changed their lives because of pain.

Compassion is often confused with pity. But when we pity someone, we see ourselves in a superior position. The immeasurable attitude of compassion arises from the recognition of our shared humanity. As Pema Chödrön explained, "Compassion is not a relationship between the healer and the wounded. It's a relationship between equals." Compassion arises in many different forms, sometimes with generosity and sometimes with boundaries. But it is always intent on removing the causes of suffering.

The Immeasurable Attitude of Empathetic Joy

The immeasurable attitude of empathetic joy, sometimes referred to as sympathetic joy, is the direct antidote to jealousy and envy. It is a straightforward, incredibly powerful tool we can cultivate and apply in our lives. Unlike the other immeasurable attitudes, empathetic joy does not require extensive explanation. Do not let this cause you to think it is of any less value.

We all know from our personal experiences how much damage results from jealousy and envy. They instantly rob us of our happiness, creating dissatisfaction and putting us at odds with others. Jealousy and envy are not limited to our feelings toward those we don't like. These emotions can arise even in regard to our dear friends and family members. When they get a wonderful relationship, land a new job, or have an amazing vacation, even if jealousy is not involved, envy can slip in. Instead of feeling our friend's joy, we can find ourselves asking, "Why not me? When will I get a great vacation or a better job?" The good news our friends share with us can cause a sense of discontentment with our own lives.

Empathetic joy is the spontaneous creation of happiness within us as a result of seeing or hearing about the wonderful and virtuous things others are doing. As with compassion, it arises from empathy, which in turn arises from the recognition of our interdependence and shared humanity. Scottish dramatist, James M. Barrie inadvertently spoke to this immeasurable attitude when he said, "Those who bring sunshine into the lives of others cannot keep it from themselves." When others are doing virtuous things, the world is more virtuous and we all benefit. When others are doing non-virtuous things, the world is less virtuous and we all suffer. As we cultivate mindfulness and observe our experiences with wisdom, we will know this to be true. To fully cultivate empathetic joy, we need to be able to truly recognize and understand our interdependence with all others.

As I illustrated in the earlier section on equanimity, everything we have in our lives, we have because of the efforts of others. This is why we begin with the immeasurable attitude of equanimity. If we can start to understand how interrelated we all are, and begin to bring an equal level of care, concern, and attention to all others, it will become easier to give them loving-kindness, have compassion for them, and experience joy for them. They have all contributed to our lives, and what we do contributes to theirs.

Unfortunately, we often forget that we don't need to compete with each other. As His Holiness, the 14th Dalai Lama reminds us, "The goal is not to be better than the other man, but your previous self."

We need only concern ourselves with having something to contribute. A classic example of this can be found in business—especially if it is our business. We can be very unhappy if we see people are successful in the same business as ours and providing the same services as ours. If we find our business is valuable and offers something to the world, wouldn't it be quite natural to be happy that others are benefiting from this service even when provided by others? Or should we be happy they are benefiting from the service only when we are providing it?

A friend of mine who teaches yoga shared with me the difficulty she has had teaching at different studios. One studio would not allow her to teach at any of the others in town or allow her to facilitate workshops for any of the others. It seems in that particular town there is a lot of competition for clients and some actual hostility among the studios. Instead of being joyful to know there are others teaching yoga and helping people heal by meeting their physical and emotional needs, the studio managers became resentful of each other. It might be more fruitful to focus on meeting the needs of one's own clients instead of worrying about what others are doing.

While I'm using yoga in this example, this scenario is common across all forms of business, and even in spiritual communities. If we can cultivate empathetic joy, we can rejoice in the fact that others are getting their needs met. To be clear, empathetic joy is taking joy specifically in the virtuous and wonderful things that people are doing. It is not a frivolous joy that sees all things as inherently good. If we mistakenly get caught up in such a frivolous joy, we are unable to recognize and address the unhealthy and harmful things that are going on in the world.

As is true with all of the concepts and principles discussed so far in this book, developing the immeasurable attitude of empathetic joy requires effort and practice. We need to be mindful of our interactions with others and notice as quickly as possible when jealousy or envy arises. When we hear good news, whether about our friends and family or strangers, we need to make a conscious effort to reflect on how wonderful it is for them. Try to bring to mind how important it is to water the seeds of joy instead of the weeds of jealousy or envy.

A good example of the immeasurable attitude of empathetic joy is the happiness we feel when our children do well. It is the joy that arises as they take their first steps, share their toys, or do well in school. We have a deep connection to our family members and, if we have healthy relationships with them, it is easy to have such joy.

The practice of developing empathetic joy starts with striving to extend that connection to others. Take time to reflect on how even the people we don't like are able to contribute beneficially to us all. They may have been the ones who drove the trucks that delivered the food we are eating today. Try to take some time every day to cultivate empathy through the short and simple reflection we discussed in the section on equanimity.

Just like me, all others are trying to be happy.

Just like me, all others are trying to avoid suffering.

Just like me, all others have known sadness and despair.

Just like me, all others are trying to meet their needs.

Just like me, all others are learning how to live.

Chapter Eight

Taking Action

"An ounce of practice is worth more than tons of preaching."
Mahatma Gandhi

We have covered quite a bit of ground to this point. I do hope what you've read thus far has been relevant, inspiring, and ultimately beneficial. While I personally do not claim any great wisdom, the wisdom and teachings in this book have permeated my life, transforming it into a truly meaningful one.

I have had the incredible good fortune to have wonderful teachers who came in all shapes and sizes. It is their wisdom, not mine, that allowed me to climb out of the depths of self-inflicted suffering and into the land of conscious living. They taught me how to train my attention and tame my unruly mind; to let go of delusional stories, labels, and elaborations, and learn to see the world more accurately; to distinguish between the thoughts, habits, and tendencies in my life that create suffering and the ones that create genuine happiness. They also taught me that *knowing* all of this may not make a bit of difference in my life.

Having knowledge is not the same as using it. Knowledge itself does not improve, much less transform a life. As my dear friend Dusty often says, "You can starve reading a cookbook." It is only when we put our knowledge into action that it becomes meaningful. A useful analogy involves receiving the proper medicine from a doctor. Even if we have access to a highly qualified doctor who can precisely diagnose our ailment and provide us with the medicine we need, it will be of no help unless we actually take the medicine as directed.

How many times have you been inspired to change your life? Maybe you attended a talk, workshop, or retreat that provided the answers you are looking for, inspiring you to start living differently. Possibly you took a course or read a book that resonated with the way you would like to live your life. What about New Year's resolutions wherein you've vowed to make desired changes?

We have all faced deeply challenging events that caused us to pause and reflect on the meaning of our lives and how we would like to live differently. Throughout our lives we have received valuable lessons and have had opportunities to improve the quality of our lives. Sometimes we took advantage of those lessons and sometimes we did not. Sometimes we put our best efforts forward only to slowly slide back into our old habits—this is the most common scenario.

Our habits and conditioning are strong. They have been developed over many years and are entrenched within us. They are like a marble in a well-worn groove. Though we may push the marble out and decide to live life differently, soon it falls back into the groove and we are again following our old patterns. This often leads us to believe we cannot change. Of course, this is absolutely not true. As I pointed out earlier, we (all of us) are always changing. The question is: Do we change consciously, establishing healthy habits, free will, and a meaningful life, or do we change unconsciously?

We can change consciously, but it requires ongoing effort. We need to push the marble out of the old groove every day. Sure, it will fall back into the groove again and again; our habits and conditioning do not change easily. However, we can push the marble out over and over. As we do this with attention and intention in our lives, the marble will stay out of the groove a little longer each time and eventually start to wear a new groove. This new groove is created with effort and persistence. It can be filled with healthy habits that support the life we choose, helping us become the people we want to be, and live in a way we define as meaningful.

Sometimes the life you want to live and the person you want to be can seem far removed, if not unobtainable. It can seem as if there is an overwhelming amount of work to do and so much to overcome. It is true no magic pill exists that can give us the life we want. It is also true that a meaningful life and the person we want to be is available to each of us in every moment of our life. In fact, the only life that truly exists is in the present moment—this moment.

The past is gone, and the future is yet to arise. The time to improve our life is always now. You can be the person you want to be right now. Make whatever you are doing meaningful, and you are living a meaningful life right now. Instead of seeing the life you want to live in the distant future, just start living the life you want today. It is really that simple, and that challenging. The only one standing in your way is you.

When I was growing up, my family did not have much money. My dad died when I was six years old and my mother, an amazing woman, had to raise nine children by herself. I was number eight. My mother worked hard, attended evening courses, rode the bus, and made sure all of us had enough to eat and got to school on time. She wanted us to have the same opportunities everyone else had, and she made sure we were able to participate in activities such as swimming and Little League.

While playing Little League, I met kids and had friends who came from families with a lot of money. Sometimes they would have team parties and other activities at their homes. Some of those homes were amazing. Many were large and beautiful and had swimming pools. As wonderful as those homes were, one of the things that really stood out for me was blue toilet water. For some reason, I thought it was great to have deep blue water in the toilet. We did not have blue toilet water, and I saw it only in the bathrooms at the homes of my wealthier friends. My mind associated blue toilet water with rich people, and I never even imagined that I could have it.

Over the years, I would have many other experiences with blue toilet water. I would see it in commercials on television and even in the average homes of people I would meet. I thought the commercials were great and always loved the opportunity to use a toilet with blue water. Still, it never occurred to me that I could have blue toilet water. For some reason, in my mind, that was for people who were much better than me.

Eventually, I would enter into recovery and become a responsible member of society. As I mentioned earlier, I got a job at the auto parts store, moved into a studio apartment, and bought a 1969 Plymouth. I was learning how to live and finding my way. There was so much to learn and, fortunately, I had a lot of support from people in the recovery community. They helped me get a checking account and taught me how to apply for a check-cashing card at the local grocery store.

One day I was at the grocery store doing my shopping, and (you won't believe this) I came upon tablets that make blue toilet water. It was right there on Aisle 5. Even more amazing, it cost less than a dollar. I was stunned and excited all at once. Here I was, armed with a checking account and a check-cashing card, able to fulfill my lifelong dream of having blue toilet water. I immediately put two containers into my cart, hurried through the rest of my shopping and headed home. As soon as I got there, even before I put the rest of the groceries away, I put both containers into the toilet reservoir and flushed the toilet. Lo and behold, I finally had my own blue toilet water!

Now this may sound silly to you. Also, for the record, I am not recommending the use of such chemicals in toilets; I don't know how healthy or unhealthy they are for the environment, but I suspect they are harmful. I tell this story because it became a much greater life lesson and a profound revelation for me. Just as the blue toilet water was always on Aisle 5, the life I had always wanted was always accessible to me. The blue toilet water is not only for wealthy people and neither is a meaningful life. The perceptions, conditioning, assumptions, and beliefs I had held in my mind prevented me from realizing that blue toilet water was actually inexpensive and easy to obtain. Even though I had seen many commercials for it, had walked down grocery store aisles that carried it, and had seen it in the homes of many others, my mind had prevented me from realizing how accessible it was. That struck me as phenomenal and prompted this question: What else is my mind preventing me from seeing and understanding?

Over time, I've discovered my mind—with its obsessive, compulsive, and delusional nature—has been the biggest obstacle in my life, much greater than any tragedy or hardship I have experienced. To be clear, I am not talking about the outer circumstances of my life. Having blue toilet water or not was not the real issue. The real issue was that I did not believe myself to be worthy of acquiring such a thing. Likewise, we need to realize we are worthy of a meaningful life and that it is accessible in every moment. Again, the only thing that separates the person you are from the person you want to be is the action you take.

There's an old bit of wisdom that states, "You cannot simply think yourself into right living, you must live yourself into right thinking." This is an important reminder of the transformative power of taking action. Every journey begins with the first step, and every step we take with attention and intention makes a difference. Sitting around thinking and talking about becoming a better person does not make you a better person.

If we want inner peace, contentment, and meaning in our life, we need to create the causes for them. Those causes are consistently found in the here and now. If we continually engage in the moments of our lives, remembering their true value, every day can be a meaningful day. In the same way that people accumulate many years in recovery by staying clean "one day at a time," our meaningful days add up to meaningful weeks, months, years, and a lifetime.

About fifteen years ago, the messiness of life once again rose up and confronted me. I was getting my teaching credential and it was my final year of college. My marriage had come apart under difficult circumstances, and I was once again a single parent. The separation and divorce were emotionally difficult for my daughter and me. The life we had planned had suddenly vanished. I had quit my high-paying corporate job to return to school and now had to scramble, working three jobs to pay the bills. My daughter was in her last year of high school and we lived a simple life in a small duplex.

Fortunately, I already had fifteen years of recovery and mindful living under my belt. So even though I would experience waves of sadness, confusion, and depression, I knew they were temporary. Even though life was difficult, it never felt hopeless. Because of the kindness, wisdom, and support of my dear teachers and wonderful friends, I always knew that each day was a new opportunity.

Even in the midst of pain, it was actually a very hopeful time for me and my daughter. We even talked about new dreams and the future we would like to create. My daughter wanted to attend college in San Francisco and become a social worker. I wanted to finish my teaching credential and someday be able to take disadvantaged kids on a trip to Europe. Even though those dreams seemed out of reach at the time, we both decided they were worthwhile and we headed in those directions.

We followed a path articulated by Saint Francis of Assisi: "Start by doing what is necessary, then what is possible, and suddenly you are doing the impossible." First, we needed to do what was necessary. Initially, that was paying the bills. My daughter got a part-time job. I returned to work as an auto mechanic, cleaned carpets on the side, and did the bookkeeping for my friend's plumbing business. I had to meet with my professors to explain my new circumstances, and they were kind enough to allow me extra time to turn in my assignments. My daughter focused on her schoolwork and studied for her college entrance exams.

We then started focusing on what was possible. Though we did not have much money and could barely make ends meet, my daughter applied to universities and for financial aid. I finished my degree and applied for an emergency teaching credential in social studies, which would allow me to teach in a public school while I was still in the credentialing program. When I contacted the Los Angeles Unified School District, they told me there was an abundance of fully credentialed social study teachers so I should not bother applying. I decided to submit my paperwork anyway, and then started sending my resume to individual schools within the district.

Now for the impossible. Even though we did not have money for college, my daughter was accepted at a university in San Francisco. She received some grants and loans and I was able to provide some money to get her started. She would have to work throughout her college career. At one point, she was injured and became disabled. Instead of giving up, she switched positions at work and was able to continue her employment. Essentially, she was able to put herself through school and graduate with a bachelor's degree in social work. She then applied for the master's degree program in social work and was one of the youngest people ever accepted. She also qualified for a state program that paid for her master's degree education in return for two years of service as a social worker. She continues to work as a social worker and now has a wonderful husband and two precious daughters.

I was offered a job with my emergency credential. I was able to be paid as a teacher while I finished my credential program. After my daughter moved to the San Francisco Bay area, my goal was to live and teach in Long Beach, California, where a friend had offered me a lovely place to live. This meant I would either have to commute about an hour and a half each way to work in Los Angeles or get a new teaching position in Long Beach. Once again knowing the odds were against me, I applied to the Long Beach School District and submitted my resume to the individual schools there. I was offered a position that I would come to love at Jordan High School. The school was perfect for me. It was right on the border of North Long Beach, Compton, and Paramount, and the students were mostly minorities from low-income families. They inspired me so much that I embarked on the other part of my dream: bringing students to Europe.

I had never been to Europe. One of my close friends, who was also a schoolteacher, had taken her students on an educational trip to Europe and that had sparked my dream years earlier during my divorce. I contacted a tour company and worked with them to facilitate a student trip. Because my students did not have the financial resources to pay for such a trip, we had to raise funds. We started our own business at a kiosk at the marina. The students all learned how to run it and worked shifts. We started our own coffee shop at the high school. The students learned valuable business and marketing skills. We worked during the summer, before and after school, and on weekends. We organized car washes and sold firewood. All of these enterprises would pay off through our collective efforts, and I ended up being able to take students to Europe two years in a row.

When my daughter and I were struggling with our emotions and working through the transition of a divorce, we had no idea how our lives would turn out. We had dreams that seemed worthwhile, even if they seemed unreachable at the time. Ultimately, we did not have power over how things would turn out. Myriad circumstances and conditions could have gone any number of ways. What we did have control over were the actions we took. We charted a direction but paid attention to each step on the path. Whether or not we would ultimately wind up at our chosen destination or a different one was not nearly as important as the journey itself. The journey was filled with difficulties, hardships, joys, and laughter. We did not suspend our happiness until some future date when our goals would be met. We tried our best to engage in every day, sometimes failing miserably, but trying to remember that each moment was a new opportunity to be the people we wanted to be.

The other dream we had that came to fruition was to have my daughter's half-sister become a part of our lives. Though officially she lived in foster care, she was able to spend summers and Christmas holidays with us. She became my second daughter, and when she turned eighteen she was able to join our family full time.

As I share stories from my personal life here, I want to remind you that I am also still a work in progress. My years of learning have been filled with many mistakes and struggles. It is not as if I simply decided to change my life and that was that. It is much more accurate to say I knew I needed to change my life, I was willing to become teachable, and I tried my best to apply what I was taught. In doing so, I have been able to participate in a life I never could have imagined.

Your life contains opportunities and potential that are unseen and often beyond your imagination. However, the opportunities and potential do not arise simply from thinking about them. They arise dependent upon, and in direct relationship to, the actions you take and the way you engage in your life. As the famed psychologist Carl Jung stated, "You are what you do, not what you say you'll do." Your past not need dictate your future, but what you do today can consciously shape your future. Living this day, and each day thereafter, actively engaged in meaningful activities, creates a meaningful life.

CHAPTER NINE
Living Mindfully

"Excellence is an art won by training and habituation. We do not act rightly because we have virtue or excellence, but we rather have those because we have acted rightly. We are what we repeatedly do. Excellence, then, is not an act but a habit." ARISTOTLE

The most powerful way to cultivate the wisdom of a meaningful life is to develop a daily mindfulness practice. There are five tools that can help you become successful. You will find that each, on its own, is beneficial. Together they are transformative. Developing and strengthening these tools in your life will significantly increase your ability to establish and sustain a mindful, and in turn, meaningful life.

Resolve: Develop a firm resolution to live a meaningful life. This is done by continually calling to mind the incredible opportunities and resources you have and remembering that you won't have them forever. Your life, like all things, is impermanent. This day is truly precious for it will never come again. Every day brings you opportunity and brings you closer to your inevitable death. Remembering this, resolve to live each day with attention and intention, for it will never come again. You are worth it.

Habit: Develop supportive rituals and routines. As I've mentioned throughout this book, what we water grows. You can develop healthy habits that support and sustain the life you want. As illustrated by the analogy of the marble in a well-worn groove, our current habits and tendencies are strong. We need to make a conscious effort to create and sustain new habits. Over time, with sustained effort, they can become as effortless as the habits we already have. Creating the habit of a structured daily meditation and mindfulness practice, which I will describe in detail, can truly transform your life.

Merit: Learn how to transform every event and interaction in your life into a cause for genuine happiness. Every moment of our life is a meaningful one, offering us the opportunity to develop our highest potentials. In all things that happen, we can continually ask this most important question: What is the most beneficial thing I can do? How can I respond in a way that is in alignment with my values and serves the greater good? Whether you break your leg, win an award, get married, or lose a dear friend, you have the opportunity to cultivate happiness.

Selflessness: Abandon the misperception of being the center of the universe. Let go of the persistent delusion that you are an independent being. Remember all life, including yours, is interdependent. As discussed earlier, everything we have, know, and are able to do is dependent on others, as are all of the causes and conditions that gave rise to the life we have. Also, remember that however you perceive yourself, you are changing all the time. You can continually grow and cultivate the qualities in your life that you find beneficial and meaningful.

Intentional activity: Consciously cultivate your values, motivation, and beneficial mental states such as the four immeasurable attitudes. Instead of allowing your mind to unconsciously drag you from one thought to another, consciously bring to mind the person you want to be and the life you want to live. Set reminders around the house and at work to help you. Engage in meditations, aspirations, or prayers that help you bring your mind to healthy and altruistic states.

Establishing a Daily Mindfulness Practice

Developing and establishing a successful daily mindfulness practice starts before you go to sleep. You will find it extremely helpful to start the night before to create the conditions to start the next day. Before you go to bed create the conditions that prepare you to wake up and effortlessly begin your morning practice. For example, I set up my coffeemaker and set the timer so it is already made before my alarm goes off. I have the clothes I'm going to wear set out and my meditation area ready. Take some time to reflect on the way you would like to start your day.

How much time do you need to set aside to meditate, reflect, and prepare for your day? Decide on the best time for you to wake up, allowing for a successful morning. When you set your alarm, set a strong intention to wake up at that time. Remind yourself why you are choosing to get up at that time and why it is important for you. I usually take a little time to visualize myself turning off the alarm, taking a moment in bed to set my intention to live mindfully, getting out of bed, and then heading down the hallway toward the coffeepot. I have found over the years that if I take the time to do this before I go to sleep, there is a much greater probability that I will actually get up on time and do my morning practice.

One of the most valuable things we can do to support living mindfully is to start shaping our motivation as quickly as possible upon awakening. As we wake up, our mind can quickly start creating lists of things to do or things to avoid doing. So before the mind can take over, it is important to start setting your intentions by bringing to mind how you would like to consciously engage in this day that will never come again. I recommend having a little reminder note right by your bedside that you can access right away, with something written on it that you find inspiring. My wife has a wall hanging with a thoughtful quote by His Holiness the

14ᵗʰ Dalai Lama titled, A Precious Human Life. It reminds her of how fortunate she is to have the life that she does and to be movitated to use it wisely, developing herself and using the day to live with purpose and meaning. She can see this easily as she gets out of bed in the morning.

I have established a little habit of wiggling my toes upon awakening. This reminds me to take a moment and call to mind that I am alive. I have another opportunity to participate in the miracle of life. As I get out of bed and place my feet on the floor, I consciously see myself stepping into a new day. This is a habit that helps me immediately start living mindfully and begin to shape my motivation for participating in this day that will never come again. I encourage you to find a method that works well for you.

Try to be as mindful as you can as you go about your morning routine, whether it's brushing your teeth or taking a shower, try to be as present as possible in your activities without allowing your mind to get busy. It can be helpful to bring intention into your activities as well. For example, when brushing your teeth, call to mind the benefits of brushing your teeth and how it will help sustain the life you want to live. Then attend to the process of brushing your teeth consciously and thoughtfully, instead of going through the motions of brushing your teeth while letting your mind wander off on tangents.

After your morning routine, with your mind alert, settle in for your formal morning practice. Get comfortable and relaxed and take some time to set your motivation for the day.

I encourage reflecting on the following three areas to help you set your intention for the day:

1. **Gratitude.** Take a little time to call to mind all of the opportunities and resources you have in your life. So many people in this world don't have access to education, electricity, or even running water in their homes. Reflect on all the things you have to be grateful for, the resources you have, the opportunities available to you, your friends and relationships, family, and so on.

Try to make this list relevant and fresh each day. Call to mind, as accurately as you can, an assessment of the incredible potential you have available to you and all of those people and resources that make your life possible.

2. **Impermanence.** Having called to mind the incredible life you have and the opportunities available to you, it is then important to remember its impermanent nature. We have all of this available to us right now, but it will not last forever. As I noted earlier, there are two things we do know about death: Death is certain, and the time of death is uncertain. Again, I do not bring this up as a morbid thought, but as a reminder to inspire us not to waste this day that will never come again. In truth, we don't know that we will be here tomorrow. How much do we put off until tomorrow? By making peace with our inevitable death, we are empowered to fully live our lives. Take a little time to reflect on all those people you know who have died. Some died very young, some when they were very old, some very quickly, some very slowly. The point of this reflection is to remind us of the urgency of the life we have now. Do not take it for granted by putting off developing the qualities you would like to have in yourself and the life you would like to engage in.

3. **Motivation.** You have a rare and precious life, one that only a small percent of the seven billion other humans on this planet have—but you won't have it forever. Each day brings us all closer to our death. I invite you to call to mind this question: What will be truly important to me at the time of my death? Will it be all the things you worry about and stress over every day? Are the resentments and agitations that arise in daily activities going to be important? Over many years, a common answer tends to arise, regardless of an individual's culture or spiritual tradition: What matters at the time of death is how we lived our lives. What are the seeds you would like to plant in the life you want to grow?

What are the qualities you would like to develop in yourself and how do you want to live this day that will never come again? Take some time to firmly cultivate a resolve to not waste this day, and to do your best to live it in a way you find meaningful.

Having taken some time to reflect on your life and how you would like to participate in the day, call to mind the importance of developing attention in your life. By learning to train our minds and cultivate our attention, we create the opportunity to establish and grow free will in our lives. This is the antidote to our biggest obstacle: the obsessive and compulsive mind. As discussed earlier, one of the most effective ways to cultivate attention is the regular practice of shamatha meditation—detailed in Chapter Four. Decide on an appropriate amount of time to meditate, set a timer, and begin meditating.

At the conclusion of your meditation, take a little time to reflect on a specific quality or skill you would like to develop today. Set an intention to live today as mindfully as possible and to specifically cultivate the quality you've chosen. It could be patience, equanimity, attention, kindness, or another value that is important to you.

The next step can be done in a variety of ways, and I encourage you to find the method that works best for you. Essentially, this step involves writing down your intention for the day on a piece of paper or in a journal, and checking in several times during the day to note how well you are doing, both with your intention and with cultivating genuine happiness.

I used to carry a piece of paper with me that I could easily fold up in my pocket. I would write the date and my intention at the top, then select six times during the day to stop and check in. Then I would write my actual check-in times on my piece of paper. This worked well for me because I was a schoolteacher on a schedule, so I knew the best times to stop and check in. A piece of paper in my back pocket was easy to access. I would also use it as a to-do list so I would reference it frequently and be reminded to check in. These days, I carry a little journal around and use that instead. Some people find it easier to use their phones. There are many mindfulness and journaling apps available that help make such checking in easy.

As you participate in your day, try to be as mindful as possible, observing your actions, reactions, thoughts, and feelings. Maintain your intention as much as possible and try to cultivate the causes of genuine happiness in all of your activities.

I suggest that you check in between three and six times a day. At the designated check-in time, take a moment to pause, relax, and take a few breaths to clear your mind. Reflect on the past few hours and note what you have been doing skillfully. By skillfully, I mean in a way that is in alignment with your values and is beneficial or nurtures the particular intention you established for the day. Also take time to reflect on and note any unskillful actions you have engaged in. It is extremely valuable to write these things on your piece of paper or in your journal, or note them with whatever technology you're using. There is a big difference between just mentally noting them and actually writing them down. Take a moment now and consider how much you can forget in a day. When you write down things or note them using your preferred technology, you can refer to them at the end of the day. This whole pause-and-reflect activity does not need to take longer than a minute or two. This is not a journaling session, just a quick check-in and a note for you to refer to later. It can be difficult to establish new habits, and the easier this process is, the more likely it is that you can and will utilize it.

This is the essence of mindfulness practice—becoming a conscious participant in your own life. You can start becoming aware of your motives as well as your actions, and what is happening internally as well as externally. As you bring awareness into your activities, you will be able to notice your healthy actions, habits, and tendencies in addition to those that are unhealthy. This is the heart of the practice, gaining insight into the sources of genuine happiness and suffering in your daily life.

At the end of the day, take a little time to reflect. Refer to the notes about skillful and unskillful actions you collected during the day. I encourage you to take a little time to call to mind how powerful your skillful actions were and how you would like to continue to nourish them in your life. Note how your skillful actions aligned with your values. Then, take some time to call to mind your unskillful actions. In what ways were they detrimental? How did they go against your personal values? How could you have responded in a more beneficial way?

When you are reflecting on your activities, remember to be gentle with yourself. This is a practice, and we need to understand that even the effort to become a better person makes you a better person. As I mentioned earlier, there is no benefit in beating up ourselves or being overly hard on ourselves. This is a time to clearly bring awareness into how we are living our life and how we would like to improve it. You deserve all the love, kindness, and compassion you seek to bring to others.

If there is a particular event you do not feel good about and would like to learn from and change, I suggest you do the following meditation on *Transforming Unskillful Events*. This is a wonderful wisdom practice and a powerful method to change our unskillful habits and tendencies into skillful ones. Whether or not you engage in the meditation, it is extremely helpful to take a little time to reflect on, and identify, how your feelings and the unskillful event were related to any or all of the three misperceptions in Chapter Six. It is ideal to do this before the meditation.

Transforming Unskillful Events Meditation

Take a few moments to relax and breathe. Bring all of you awareness into your body and rest your awareness there. Relax any tension you find in your body. Let each in-breath be an invitation to relax. Let each out-breath be an opportunity to release—letting go of any and all tensions, worries, or concerns. Breathing in, relax. Breathing out, release. Do this until you are relaxed and centered.

Now take a moment to set a strong motivation for engaging in this precious opportunity to transform your life. Set the motivation to be compassionate with yourself and with others. Remember you are taking the time to participate in your life in a meaningful way. So take a moment to clearly establish your motivation, to participate in this meditation, to transform and improve the quality of your interactions with others, and to make your life meaningful.

Now call to mind that life is messy and all of us have done things we feel good about, as well as things we don't feel so good about. Remember all others are just like you, trying to find happiness, trying to avoid suffering. All others also know despair and sadness. They're trying to have their needs met. And just like you, they are learning how to live. We are all in this together, doing the best we can with what we have.

Now call to mind a situation you would like to transform. A situation in which you didn't feel good about your interaction. It could be an event, an activity with others, or just a continuous mental habit. Take a moment to call it to mind as clearly as possible, as though you are watching the scene in front of you. Keep in mind that all parties in the scene are doing the best they can with what they have. Step back from the scene and observe it. What can you learn about yourself? What was triggered? What is your sense of the needs of the others involved? Step back from the scene and see what you can learn about what happened. What's the inner cause that provoked your unskillful response? In what way was this situation harmful to you or others?

Having gained insight into this unskillful event, how could you have responded more skillfully? How could you have responded in a way that was more beneficial? How would you like to respond the next time this situation happens? Take a moment to strongly call to mind the way you would like to respond in the future. See yourself responding in this way. How could the outcome be different? Now set a firm intention that whenever a situation like this arises again, you will do your best to respond in the more skillful way. Take moment to set this firm intention.

CHAPTER TEN

The Wisdom of a Meaningful Life

"You can't cross the sea merely by standing and staring at the water."
RABINDRANATH TAGORE

Living a meaningful life is both the essence and the fruit of living a mindful life. They are inseparable. There is no way to live a meaningful life without attention and intention. Likewise, when we develop the four keys of living mindfully—attention, values, wisdom, and an open heart—our life becomes meaningful.

As discussed in Chapter One, mindfulness is not an isolated skill. It is embedded in many invaluable teachings on liberation from suffering. Mindfulness is an insight practice that can provide us with opportunities to experience ourselves and the world more accurately. Mindfulness empowers us to stop engaging in activities that create suffering and start engaging in those that give rise to genuine happiness.

It comes as no surprise that to truly benefit from all that mindfulness has to offer, we need to *live* mindfully. Our mindfulness practice (while still helpful) will be limited if we think of it only in terms of mindfulness meditation and learning to be more present in the moments of our life. To unlock its full potential and transformative power, we need to develop mindfulness in the context of the three higher trainings of virtue, meditation, and wisdom, and infuse it with the four immeasurable attitudes that open the heart.

My goal in writing this book is to share with you the wisdom of my teachers and present a method of living mindfully that includes its full potential in a way that is practical, accessible, and universal:

- *Practical* in that you can see how to apply these teachings. These teachings are not meant to be philosophical; they are meant to be applied in our daily life in ways that are effective and produce results.
- *Accessible* in that these teachings are understandable; that the concepts are presented with clear examples and explained in ways that makes sense.
- *Universal* in that they apply to everyone. This was most important to me. Although Buddhist in origin, the teaching of mindfulness is a universal wisdom that can help everyone become a better version of themselves, whoever and whatever they are. The cultivation of ethics, concentration, wisdom, and an open heart are not unique to Buddhists; these teachings can be found in all spiritual and many philosophical traditions. I wanted to present them in a way that can empower people, regardless of their culture, spiritual beliefs, philosophy, religion, or lack of religion, to cultivate genuine happiness by engaging in their lives mindfully, in alignment with their own values.

The previous chapters provide a structure for incorporating these precious teachings into your daily life. I strongly encourage you to try to put into action whatever you have found meaningful. Our habits are strong, and sometimes it will feel as if you are swimming upstream. There will be days when the last thing on Earth you're interested in doing is being mindful. This book may be inspiring at the moment and gathering dust on a shelf later. Do not let any of these things discourage you. We do not change our habits easily, and we will have our ups and downs. There will be times of inspiration and times of laziness. Every day is a new opportunity to develop the qualities you find meaningful in your life. Every conscious moment we engage in is progress. It is never too late to change. We are changing every moment.

In addition to the daily practice instructions, I would like to offer you some specific teachings and daily activities in which you can engage. Each of these will help you develop and strengthen one of the four keys of living mindfully. In our Mindful Life Community, we offer a new teaching and support activity to members every day. We know our members, like everyone, have different needs and different levels of conscious engagement on different days. So we offer a reminder and provide support every day of the year. This way, members are able to participate in the activities they find most meaningful in regard to what is happening in their lives at any particular time.

It is our vision that as we all grow and become more skillful in our activities and interactions, we not only improve our own lives, but the lives of our families, friends, communities, and the world at large. Like ripples on a pond, our kindness can spread and flow. We can be a voice of compassion and unity, skillfully recognizing the value of all. We can all help improve the world, one mindful smile and compassionate activity at a time.

I'm including some of our daily support lessons and activities for you, some from each category of living mindfully. Please use them to supplement your daily practice. Also, it's important to know that all of the activities included are not limited to just a one-day practice. They can be more beneficial if done over a period of days, weeks, months, or even a lifetime. I do hope you find them helpful.

A MATTER OF PRACTICE
Additional Support for
Living Mindfully

Author's note: While this material has already been covered, it is important enough to review. Moreover, integrating it into defined and specific opportunities to practice applying it will deepen your learning process.

Attention

As I've described, by far, one of the biggest obstacles to finding inner peace and developing our highest potentials is our untrained mind. Unless we consciously train our mind, developing the ability to direct it where we would like it to go and attend to what we choose, it will endlessly drag us from one thought to another. The mind continuously produces thoughts and images. Again, try to not think for one full minute and see what happens.

It's one thing to have constant mental activity. The bigger problem is that the mind compulsively draws our attention away from what we are doing and toward the thoughts and images it produces. It tells us what to worry about and stress over, draws us in, ruminates, and projects. This is why there are times we don't know where our car keys are; our mind was somewhere else when we put them down.

If we are going to establish free will and make healthy choices, we need to be present in the moments of our lives. So much of our life goes by without our actually being present in it. How much of our day are we able to be in the present moment? At its essence, mindfulness is the ability to be fully present in the moments of our lives, attending to them with wisdom and clarity, being able to initiate actions and respond to whatever arises in ways that are healthy and meaningful to us. The first step is learning to pay attention in our own lives.

Amazing things and wondrous people constantly surround us. Unfortunately, most of the time we are too busy with distractions and our own concerns to even notice them. We tend to be the center of our own universe and pay attention primarily to people and things that directly affect us in some way. We usually focus on whether they can bring us some pleasure or will cause us some suffering. Either way, it is about us. Rather than promoting opportunities to find joy in our activities, our self-centered way of living creates stress and worry as we constantly try to avoid suffering and find pleasure.

When we are able to shift our attention away from ourselves, becoming members of this wondrous universe instead of its center, our stress and worries can fade away and give rise to our more natural, curious, and joyful mind. The act of becoming aware of something as simple as our feet on the ground in this moment provides an anchor for our attention that allows us to let go of our busy mind and find peace. Actually, the peace is always there. It is usually covered up with our obsessive-compulsive mind. You'll notice whenever you are fully paying attention, especially to some activity you really enjoy (what some people call being in the zone or the flow) time flies and a joyful mind arises.

How often do we pay attention to the mundane activities we engage in throughout the day? Where is our mind when we are washing our hands? Did we even feel the water drops hitting our skin as we took a shower? Did we notice the trees and flowers on our way to work? Did we even notice our drive to work? If we were commuting on a busy freeway, did we remember all those other cars were filled with people just like us—with families and loved ones, worries and concerns, and personal stories of heartache and triumph? We are constantly surrounded by a wondrous world filled with incredible people. It may be worth paying attention to them.

Here are some exercises, commonly used by mindfulness teachers, I find helpful to cultivate attention and become more present in the moment.

THREE THINGS WITH THREE SENSES

- Pause and take a few breaths.
- Look around and note three things you can see.
- Listen and note three sounds you can hear.
- Notice three things you can feel with your body (e.g., the wind on your face or hands, your toes against your shoes, the ground, or a chair you are sitting in).

Try to do this with curiosity and interest. Set an intention to do this exercise as much as you can throughout the day. It would be wonderful if you could do it every hour. Even if you can do it only a few times a day, it will still be beneficial.

THREE-MINUTE MINDFULNESS

- Sit or stand up straight and relax your body.
- *First minute:* Focus all of your attention on your breath. Let the breath be natural and just focus your attention on the sensations of the breath.
- *Second minute:* Focus your attention on the physical sensations of your body.
- *Third minute:* Expand your attention by becoming aware of your surroundings. Simply observe without engaging. What do you see and hear?

Try to do this at least three times during the day.

MINDFUL WALKING

You can do this literally whenever you are walking, whether down the hall, to the car, around work, or on a stroll.

- Walk with as much awareness as possible, one step at a time.
- Be aware of each step, arrive in the present moment with each step.
- Try to be aware of the sensations of lifting, moving, and placing your feet.
- Notice how your body moves as you walk.

- Expand your awareness to your surroundings and maintain awareness of each step.
- Let you breath be natural and enjoy the walk

LABELING THOUGHTS

This is a very effective technique to reduce stress, rumination, and mind-wandering. As disruptive thoughts arise, taking your attention away from what you are doing, simply label them and let them go. For example, many thoughts about the future could be labeled as "planning." You can use labels like "fear," "remembering," or even "useful" or "unuseful." Labeling thoughts allows us to release thoughts more quickly, instead of attaching to and getting carried away by them.

You can also pick a specific mental habit or thought that is causing you problems and make that the focus of your practice. Let's use worrying as an example:

- Whenever you notice yourself worrying, simply note it with the label, "just worrying," and let it go.
- Once you label it, try to bring your awareness to your breath for a moment or two and then bring your attention to what you are doing.
- If you catch yourself worrying again, simply label it again and let go.
- It does not matter how many times you need to do this, each time is a success.

This is an extremely productive practice and one that over time allows you to let go of needless worry. Don't try to fight it or use the label "stop worrying." Simply notice worry, label it "just worrying," and let go if possible. Remember, there is an important difference between worrying and constructive problem-solving. Constructive problem-solving is helpful and productive, whereas worrying involves repetitive thoughts that usually cause anxiety with no tangible impact on the outcome we are worrying about.

NOTICE NEW THINGS

As much as possible during the day, pause and try to become aware of something you have not noticed before. So much of our surroundings go unnoticed, even in the places we spend most of our time. This practice helps you become more aware of your environment and bring your attention back into the present moment.

Values

As you become aware of your core values, begin to learn to keep them in mind, and intentionally bring them into your daily activities, you will become increasingly aware of the habits, tendencies, and beliefs that interfere with living in alignment with your values. This is the beginning of true wisdom—identifying within yourself that which prevents you from being who you really want to be.

It is important to explore ways in which we can clarify our values and bring them into our daily activities. If we can remember that living a life of integrity and in alignment with our values is the method of creating inner peace, well-being, and meaning in our lives, then it becomes imperative to consistently call to mind the person we want to be and do our best to be that person.

However, as previously noted, life is messy. This is simply the nature of things. We all have troubles, challenges, and difficulties. In times of challenge or difficulty, it can be easy to respond in ways we don't feel good about. While these times are not pleasant, they are opportunities for us to develop our highest potential and respond in ways that are truly meaningful. When we respond in a way we feel good about, we create a lasting sense of well-being. As Eleanor Roosevelt stated, "People grow through experience if they meet life honestly and courageously. This is how character is built."

One of the primary reasons people suffer in this world is because they succumb to the delusion that despite all evidence to the contrary, their lives should not be messy. Somehow, even though we know this is totally unrealistic, we can still fall into the trap of imagining that our relationships should always be wonderful, our jobs should be stable and fulfilling, we shouldn't get ill, and our family members and friends should not have problems or get divorces. When these things do happen, we are once again ill prepared and become victims of our current circumstances. So we need to be vigilant and resilient. It is our challenges and struggles that allow us to fully develop ourselves. Rarely does anyone spend a lot of time cultivating inner growth when everything is going his or her way. Take a moment to reflect on some of the challenging events in your life and recall if you responded courageously and honestly, and in alignment with your values. If you did, was this helpful? If you did not, what was the result?

VALUES ACTIVITY #1

Today, do your best to respond to any challenges that arise in a way you can feel good about tomorrow. Events and activities will come and go, but the way we respond to them leaves a lasting imprint on us.

We know change is part of the nature of everything and is inevitable. Understanding this, we can eliminate a lot of needless suffering in our lives. However, there are some things we can depend upon. For example, when we do things we feel good about, we feel good. When we act in alignment with our values, we cultivate genuine happiness—a sense of well-being that stays with us. While change in our circumstances, our relationships, jobs, health, and so many other things is an inevitable reality, we can be grateful that some things remain consistent and reliable.

The workings of gratitude are another constant; one that is well studied. The benefits of gratitude are always available to us, in any circumstance we find ourselves in. We can always be grateful for all that is going well in our lives, and for all the gifts in our lives, even amid otherwise difficult times. The benefits of gratitude are innumerable and immeasurable. So while change in our circumstances, our relationships, jobs, health, and so many other things is inevitable, we can be grateful some things remain consistent and reliable.

Values Activity #2

Throughout your day, do your best to notice those things you can depend on, such as gratitude, kindness, or honesty. Find examples of them in your day. I encourage you to reflect on what you've discovered at the end of the day. Would these be obvious to you without the focus of today's activity? Do you remember you can depend on these in your life?

Wisdom

"True freedom is the ability to respond consciously, in the most beneficial way, to whatever life throws at you."

John Bruna

One path to cultivating wisdom in our daily lives is to mindful of, and explore, the habits, tendencies, and attitudes we have developed and how they shape our interactions with others.

This will help provide some insight into recognizing and nurturing the healthy and wise choices we make, as well as acknowledging and letting go of the unhealthy ones. Ultimately, the goal is to gain wisdom, not simply acquire knowledge. With wisdom we are able to see ourselves and the world more clearly and apply the lessons we have learned in life. A good measure of our wisdom is our ability to not only be aware of healthy actions, but to actually take those actions. Obviously, this also applies to being aware of unhealthy actions and acting to avoid them. This, like many things, is much easier said than done, but with practice, our wisdom increases daily.

Wisdom Activity #1

Today, try to practice consciously changing your attitude and perspective when you encounter adverse conditions. In addition to the larger problems or disappointments that arise, I recommend that you practice on little ones such as having to wait, missing an appointment, or having to settle for a coffee or tea you don't prefer. This is a skill we can improve with practice.

When our circumstances are difficult and we have few options to change them, it is extremely helpful and productive to remember that we can change our attitude and/or our perception about them. This does not mean we simply develop a "Pollyanna" attitude, pretending everything is wonderful when it is not. That is not productive, and it can be detrimental when we don't recognize and deal with real difficulties in our lives. It is important to see things as accurately as possible so we can respond to both challenges and the opportunities with wisdom.

Having said that, circumstances, no matter how difficult, usually contain unseen opportunities and solutions. If we cannot improve our circumstances directly, we can start shifting our perspective and this may empower us to move from victims of circumstance to taking healthy solution-oriented actions. As previously discussed, our personal attitudes, expectations, and other variables, such as whether we are hungry, tired, rested, injured/sick, healthy, happy, or sad, have a direct impact on how we experience our circumstances. If we alter any of these, our experience of the circumstances changes. While we may not have the ability to change the outer circumstances, we do have the ability to change our internal ones. This is an extremely beneficial skill to develop.

WISDOM ACTIVITY #2

Today, try your best to be aware of, and note, the different emotions you feel throughout the day. Keep a notepad if you can. Try to be diligent and include even subtle ones, such as impatience, eagerness, surprise, and contentment. Notice how transient these can be.

You are not your emotions, you experience them. Your emotions will come and go and you will still be here. Realizing this, you are no longer compelled to react to them helplessly. Instead, you are empowered to respond to them with wisdom. We can feel sad and still have access to our reservoir of strength to draw upon. The circumstances and emotions will change, but the reservoir that is our genuine happiness will remain. It will, however, be affected. We will have either added to it or drained from it, depending upon how we responded.

If we understand that painful and difficult circumstances, as well as the emotions that come with them, are a natural part of life, then we can feel the feelings and be able rise to challenges with healthy actions that add to our reservoir. There are also other times when we simply need some time to draw from that reservoir. That is what it is there for. It is okay to feel good about allowing yourself to feel sad. Emotions are not who we are, they are a temporary experience we have. Instead of fighting them, we can experience them and learn from them. They are there to help us develop our wisdom, inner resources, and to connect with ourselves and others.

WISDOM ACTIVITY #3

Today, take some time to explore and test some belief about yourself that is limiting. Reflect upon a perception you have of yourself and see if it has changed over time. Even though we are changing all of the time, often our self-perceptions aren't. Challenge yourself to test a belief you have about yourself—specifically regarding something about which you perceive yourself as inadequate. See if it is still true, or not.

In general, we tend to have a strong perception of who we are: our personality type, strengths, weaknesses, skills, and limitations. We carry our self-perceptions with us day to day and instead of exploring or challenging them, we usually reinforce the beliefs we already have about ourselves. While many of our observations about ourselves are accurate, many others are based upon limited experiences and old information that is no longer valid.

We are changing all the time, whether or not we are conscious of it. Even our long held beliefs and habits, though not seeming to change, are changing and may be growing stronger. Just as a large and strong elephant can be tethered to a stake in the ground by a single rope or chain, we can be restrained by our own beliefs about ourselves. Elephants raised in captivity and used for work are often chained up this way. The reason these elephants can be restrained by something as small as a stake in the ground is because they were chained up as babies. The baby elephants learned they were not strong enough to break free and that it was painful to keep trying to free themselves. As the elephants grow and become strong enough, they maintain the belief that they are not able to free themselves and no longer try.

Just as with these elephants, many of our current perceptions are outdated, unexplored, and can stem from our childhood. It is up to us to continue to tug on and test the chains of our self-perceptions. If we do, we will find untapped abilities and potential within us. If we don't, we run the risk of unconsciously allowing those chains to limit us and keep us from developing our highest potentials.

Equanimity

"Cultivate the habit of being grateful for every good thing that comes to you, and to give thanks continuously. And because all things have contributed to your advancement, you should include all things in your gratitude." RALPH WALDO EMERSON

EQUANIMITY ACTIVITY #1

Today, I invite you to be mindful of all that you have, including the wide variety of people, opportunities, and difficulties in your life, and cultivate an appreciation and sense of gratitude for all the people and circumstances that have made your life possible. Throughout the day, check in and note if your gratitude is present.

One of the keys to cultivating equanimity is to start noticing how we exaggerate the good and bad qualities in people, events, and activities in which we are engaged. Equanimity is not indifference; rather, it is the ability to engage in all of our activities with the same level of attention and clarity whether these are difficult or joyous. It allows us to effectively deal with challenging situations and enjoy the pleasurable ones without a clinging attachment to them. With equanimity, we can bring an equality of value to all people we come in contact with, as well as all of our experiences in life. They all have something to offer.

It is easy to forget everything we have in life—our ability to read, the clothes we wear, our food, our health, etc.—is because of others. Even the annoying customer at work is the reason we have a job. We often appreciate only the things we feel good about and overlook or dismiss the things we are challenged by or don't like. It's easy to feel grateful for those individuals and experiences we know have helped us, but sometimes we don't realize how many of these there are. Upon reflection, you may find the challenges and difficult people in your life have contributed just as much as, if not more than, pleasurable people and experiences. Even people and events we experienced as negative have often been helpful to us.

To use the example from earlier, reflect on how many causes and conditions were necessary for you to have breakfast, even if it was just toast. How many people were involved in planting the wheat? How many were involved in making the tools necessary for the planting? How many were involved in harvesting? How many were involved in building and maintaining the tractors that were required? How many were involved in the buildings that were needed? How many were involved in making the building materials for the buildings? How many were involved in creating the ovens at the bakery? What about the roads on which the bread was transported and the vehicles that carried it? As you can see, this can go on and on—and this is just for a piece of bread.

EQUANIMITY ACTIVITY #2

Today, check in three times throughout your day on your view of yourself and others. Note whether your views are realistic or exaggerated in some way and whether you are putting yourself above or below someone else. Consider how your views affect your words and actions.

Pride can be one of those sneaky attitudes that initially seems helpful, but if we look a little deeper, we may find it to be quite harmful. If we look closely, we may notice that when pride shows up, we can usually trace it to an unrealistic sense of our self, an exaggerated or distorted sense of our qualities or abilities. When we notice pride in ourselves, we can see how this view places us artificially above others and brings us to devalue others in some way. Pride strengthens the common delusion that we are the center of the universe, limiting our ability to develop real concern for others, and the ability to learn from them. Similarly, low self-esteem is an exaggeration of our lack of personal qualities or abilities, and we find ourselves feeling less than others. Often, our pride actually arises from insecurity, just like our low self-esteem. As we cultivate equanimity, recognizing and valuing others and ourselves equally, the barriers of pride and low self-esteem can fall away.

When we clearly observe the reality of our strengths and abilities, as well as our weaknesses and areas where we can learn and grow, we begin to cultivate a balanced view of ourselves. Thomas Merton expressed, "Pride makes us artificial and humility makes us real." With humility, we meet others from a place of knowing we all have strengths and weaknesses and areas of knowledge and ignorance. When we dissolve the attachment to our exaggerated sense of self, we begin to dissolve our aversion for those we have thought less of. True humility results from a willingness to overcome our insecurities. Without it, our ability to learn and grow is limited, as is our ability to see all people as having value and something to teach us.

EQUANIMITY ACTIVITY #3

Today, try to extend the same compassion, kindness, and tolerance to others that you would like extended to you. Try to notice any judgments you may have about others as they arise and see how true they are when you hold them with wisdom and perspective.

If we pay attention, it can be quite startling to recognize how quickly and thoughtlessly we can judge another. One comment someone makes, a bumper sticker on their car with the different point of view, or a behavior we deem inappropriate, can cause us to instantly devalue another human being. It can be so easy to characterize another with only a few bits of knowledge about them. We actually do this all the time.

Call to mind famous people, maybe in the entertainment industry, sports, politics, or history, and you will find there are many you like and many you don't like. You may find you have strong feelings about them one way or another—even though you may have never met them and only have small fragments of information about their lives, reported by others who have only experienced limited, if any, time with them. All of these people have literally done thousands of things every day throughout all of the days of their lives. Yet, we have a judgment that we think is valid about them based upon a few things out of the entirety of their lives, that they may or may not have actually done, told to us by people who may or may not have actually been there.

With people we do know and have contact with, we can easily fall into the same trap of judging the totality of their character by some behaviors or comments we don't like. In evaluating each other, it is valuable to recognize our commonalities instead of merely focusing on another's weakness or perceived shortcoming. It is important to remember we all have strengths and weaknesses, have made mistakes and hurt people, have had success and helped people, have told lies and the truth, have been selfish and generous, have been thoughtful and thoughtless, and have been kind as well as unkind.

It is interesting that we can call someone else a liar, truly believing they are deceitful and forget that we have lied many times ourselves. In our case, that is not who we are, it is merely something we did. We don't see ourselves as deceitful. As this is true of us, it is important to remember that it is true of others. Remember, we are all trying to find happiness, get our needs met, and learn how to live. We can learn from our mistakes and improve every day, and so can others.

We are all accountable for what we do. I do not suggest you tolerate harmful activities of others, but rather I encourage you to respond to the harmful actions of others with wisdom, remembering that actions are things they do and not the person they are. Additionally, it is important to remember that if we label someone an idiot or jerk because of something he or she did or said, it is hard for us to recognize the valuable things that person has to offer today or in the future.

Loving-Kindness

"Everytime you smile at someone, it is an action of love, a gift to that person, a beautiful thing." MOTHER TERESA

LOVING-KINDNESS ACTIVITY #1

Today, try to treat everyone you meet as if they were an old dear friend. Bring as much care, kindness, and understanding into your interactions with them as possible, remembering that not one of us knows if we will still be here tomorrow.

Let's take a moment to recall the essence of loving-kindness. Loving-kindness is the deep and sincere wish for ourselves and others to be genuinely happy. It is not an attached love or kindness focused only on people we like or who are kind to us. By cultivating loving-kindness, we are cultivating the direct antidote to the mental and emotional states of anger and hatred. We cannot have love and hate for the same thing at the same time. Love can turn to hate and hate can turn to love in a moment, but they cannot exist simultaneously in the same moment. What we water grows. Wouldn't it be better to water the flowers of love and kindness instead of the weeds of anger and hatred?

Wouldn't it be wonderful if we could all treat each other with this level of concern? This is a wonderful practice that brings a depth of value to every individual with whom we come in contact. In fact, everyone has a terminal illness. It is called life. This life does not last forever, and we don't know how long anyone will be here. I cannot say this enough, everyone we meet is trying to find happiness and avoid suffering, has experienced sadness, and is trying to get his or her needs met. And, just like us, they are learning how to live. How would your attitude and actions be different if you remembered this in your daily interactions?

LOVING-KINDNESS ACTIVITY #2

Today, I invite you to practice offering loving-kindness with a smile to those you come in contact with, with as little bias or distraction as possible. Notice too, your obstacles to offering loving-kindness and set the intention to shift your habits by taking action today.

It is easy to recognize, and even feel, when someone is directing kindness or anger toward us. We know what it is like to be in a room with tension and what it is like to be greeted with a smile. It's helpful to take a moment to recall the feeling of being the recipient of a truly kind smile or action, and reflect on how that benefitted you, and what a gift it was to receive. Knowing this feeling, it seems valuable to offer such a gift to others.

Unfortunately, even if we want to, our own busyness and busy minds can prevent us from truly being present with kindness to those we come in contact with, such as a bus driver, mail carrier, receptionist, waiter or waitress, or even our partner, children, friends, and coworkers. Our busy mind can even distract us to the degree we forget that we are interacting with another precious human being. Just as our thoughts and worries can cloud our mind, so too can emotional states of anger, jealousy, sadness, anxiety, and fear. These can also cause us to be wrapped up in our own inner world and obstruct our ability to offer loving-kindness to the person in front of us.

With intention and attention, we can begin to overcome these obstacles, and begin to act with kindness more often, offering a smile, a kind word, or a kind gesture as gifts to anyone we come in contact with during our day. This kindness is palpable and affects our interactions with others on many levels. Like ripples on a pond, the kindness of a loving smile can affect a multitude of people we will never even know.

LOVING-KINDNESS ACTIVITY #3

Today, try to cultivate the attitude and action of friendliness in as many of your interactions as are appropriate. Don't wait for people to be friendly, show them how.

How often do we reserve our friendliness until we feel it is warranted by others? Do we wait, gauging the actions and intentions of others, before we deem them worthy of our friendliness? Or are we sometimes simply shy and unwilling to risk openly sharing our friendliness? Clearly, there are times when outward displays of friendliness are inappropriate or even unskillful. However, the heart and mind of friendliness is a powerful force. It can transform people, situations, and even tragedy with its care and kindness.

Too often people reserve their friendliness only for those who are friendly to them. Just as we may be waiting for them, they may be waiting for us. As the saying goes, "The best way to have friends is to be one." It can also be extremely beneficial to be friendly to those we don't care for or are challenged by. It may provide us with an opportunity to shift the relationship in ways that are healthier for all concerned. We don't need to like someone to be kind to them. In our kindness, we may recognize their value.

Compassion
COMPASSION ACTIVITY #1

Today, try your best to recognize the difference between pain and suffering. Identify the opportunities pain can offer and the suffering that arises when you try to avoid the pain you experience.

There is a saying that pain is necessary, but suffering is optional. The distinction here is that suffering is a mental state that does not want to accept pain as a part of life. Compassion always seeks to reduce suffering, so it is compassionate to learn to accept and use pain wisely, instead of always trying to avoid it.

It is perfectly reasonable and quite healthy to want to avoid pain. Unfortunately, often due to our desire to avoid legitimate pain, we wind up limiting our own personal growth and creating more suffering in the long run. In our rush to avoid pain, we usually forget that pain is a natural and often useful part of our human experience. Of course it is wise to avoid unnecessary pain, but we need to remember that pain serves a purpose. It tells us that something is wrong and needs attention. This is easy to recognize in our own body and when we hurt ourselves in some way, we know to attend to it.

In the same way, mental and emotional pain informs us of what to attend to in our own lives and helps us to make healthier choices. Our mental and emotional pain can sometimes be tricky. Although we don't want to feel sad, sadness can be an expression of our love. Our sadness can be a healthy reflection of the disappointment or loss of a loved one. Without reflection, we can fall into the delusion of thinking we should always feel good and never experience difficult emotions. As we know, this delusion can be extremely persuasive even though we, and all of the people we know, are constantly experiencing a wide range of emotions, both pleasant and unpleasant. If we can learn that our difficult emotions, just as our pleasant ones, serve a purpose, contain lessons, and are always temporary, we can learn to experience them instead of trying to avoid them. If we try to continuously protect ourselves from them, we can imprison ourselves by limiting our ability to develop our heart and connection with others.

COMPASSION ACTIVITY #2

Today, take the time to call to mind one person you would like to help and help him or her. If another appears who needs help, see if you can help that person, too.

The cultivation of compassion is dependent upon our development of empathy. Unfortunately, instead of having our empathy transform and give rise to compassion, sometimes it can get stuck and transform into hopelessness and despair. As we recognize and feel the difficulties others are experiencing, it can become overwhelming and we can feel powerless. When this happens, we are unable to see clearly that every day, everywhere in the world, the vast majority of people are engaged in countless healthy and meaningful activities that make the world a better place. For every bit of harm done, there are thousands of kind, or at least neutral, activities taking place. However, these do not become news headlines and often do not make an impression in our own minds. As the American television personality and educator, Fred Rogers always pointed out in the face of tragedy, "Look for the helpers. You will always find people who are helping."

There have always been those who need help and those who give help. Sometimes we are the ones in need of help and other times we are the helper. It is in this giving and receiving that our humanity is shared and our highest potential is reached. It is important to recognize and remember this so that our empathy transforms into the action of compassion instead of hopelessness and despair. Mother Teresa was an incredible example of this, and she always reminded us that it all begins with helping the one in front of us.

COMPASSION ACTIVITY #3

Today, remember every moment is a new opportunity for you to be the person you want to be. Let your past inform you, but not restrain you. Start today, to find even small ways to improve the world around you through your actions.

Every moment we have in life is an opportunity to improve ourselves and the world we live in. No matter what has happened, whether it was years ago or moments ago, this new moment offers us new opportunities. We need not let our past dictate our future. Each day we have a fresh start—if we are able to let go of old habits and tendencies and choose to embrace the opportunities in front of us in the new moments of our lives. The time to improve yourself is always now. In fact, it is the only time in which we can engage in meaningful activities and consciously cultivate the qualities we want to develop in our lives.

You can be the person you want to be right now. In this moment, in whatever situation arises, if you are mindful, you have an opportunity to engage in it in a way that honors your values. We may not always respond or act in skillful and meaningful ways. But as soon as we realize this, we have a choice to improve ourselves. One of the keys is to remember that no matter how unskillful we may have been, at that moment, we did the best we could. Generally, we never purposely try to make mistakes or ruin our lives. Given the situation, our emotions, and level of personal development at that moment, we acted or reacted in the only way we could. If we can remember this, we can be gentle with ourselves and learn from our missteps. They provide us with the life lessons that empower us to make wiser choices in the new moments of our lives.

Every time you cultivate healthy, beneficial thoughts and engage in compassionate activities that alleviate suffering, either for yourself or others, you make the world a better place. Every moment offers opportunities to alleviate suffering and cultivate genuine happiness if you are aware of them.

Empathetic Joy

"Appreciation is a wonderful thing: It makes what is excellent in others belong to us as well." VOLTAIRE

Empathetic Joy Activity

Today is a day to practice empathetic joy for others, rejoicing in their virtuous activities and successes. We can do this by engaging and supporting others in activities that bring them joy, fulfillment, and satisfaction or by simply being happy for them. When you hear of another person experiencing joy because of an experience, situation, or achievement, celebrate and share that joy with him or her, even if the event has no relevance for you or is not a preference of yours.

When we feel truly connected to others and understand that everyone contributes to the conditions that give rise to this thing we call life, a heartfelt joy will arise within us when we see or hear of others doing well. This is the same kind of joy felt by parents when their child does something special. Just as parents are connected to their children, we are all connected to each other. This can be easy to forget due both to the pervasive messages in American culture about the importance of being independent, and the delusions and exaggerations with which our minds can become preoccupied. When we forget our connection with others and focus only on our own needs and desires, we sow the seeds of competition, jealousy, and envy. Whether consciously or not, our mind constantly evaluates how well we are doing in relation to others, creating dissatisfaction and division.

However, if we can abandon our misdirected, self-centered thoughts and desires and remember the true nature of the world we live in, we will find an immeasurable amount of joy in the world around us. When others do amazing things, the world is a more amazing place. When others do virtuous things, the world is a more virtuous place. When others create wondrous things, the world is a more wondrous place. When others do kind things, the world is a kinder place. When others do loving things, the world is a more loving place.

We all benefit from the compassionate and virtuous accomplishments of others. Remembering that all others help us in some way and that, just like us, they have known hardship and despair, we can develop our connection with and empathy for them. We are all part of the same family—a family of human beings trying to find our way, looking for happiness, and trying to avoid suffering. When we rejoice in the virtues of others, we cultivate empathetic joy and eliminate the seeds of envy and jealousy.

Action

"All life is an experiment. The more experiments you make the better." RALPH WALDO EMERSON

TAKING ACTION ACTIVITY #1

Today, reflect upon some small insecurities that prevent you from participating more fully and authentically in your life. Make a choice to not succumb to them today. Engage in some experiments you are a little uncomfortable with.

There is no better teacher than experience. Unfortunately, our fears and insecurities frequently prevent us from gaining valuable experience. It can be challenging to risk making mistakes, failing, or looking foolish. Sometimes fear around financial and significant life changes prevents us from really stepping into our lives. Sometimes insecurities or concerns about how others view us prevent us from engaging in life authentically. It is easy to become preoccupied with the outer circumstances of our lives, our social and economic standing, and how others see us. However, instead of creating inner confidence and well-being, this usually creates more insecurity and dissatisfaction.

Imagine what your life would be like and what decisions you would make if you had no insecurities. How would your life be different? How would your choices be different? What would happen if you simply showed up every day, did the best you could, and did not worry about the outcome or what others think? No need to worry about making mistakes, everyone does. No need to worry about looking foolish at times, everyone does. No need to worry about failing, everyone does. In fact, you have many times. We learn by doing, and often we learn much more by failing.

Ultimately, we can only do our best. The outcomes are out of our control. It is important to remember that it is difficult to do our best when we are unwilling to try new things or afraid to make mistakes. Emerson's quote on the previous page invites us to fully engage in our lives, authentically and fearlessly. Fearlessly does not mean in absence of fear, but an unwillingness to succumb to it. It means that when we are nervous, anxious, or fearful, we are still willing to take the healthy actions that make our lives meaningful. It does not mean we should not feel fear or that we should be reckless in our thoughts or behavior. I encourage you to take small steps, working on small fears and insecurities that prevent you from engaging in the great experiment that we call life.

TAKING ACTION ACTIVITY #2

Today, I invite you to take some time and reflect upon a particular mental affliction that you would like to work on, such as impatience, judgment, stress, or insecurity. Take a little time to examine how unhelpful it is for you. Make a conscious decision to do your best to not succumb to it today. Keep this choice in mind, and when the mental state arises, do your best to recognize it and let it go. Remember, it is simply a temporary mental or emotional state. You have had them many times and they always have come and gone. There is no need to concern yourself with how well you do it or not. It is a practice and merely being aware of it in your daily life is extremely helpful.

Meditation is an exceptionally valuable tool in providing us with mental stability, perspective, inner peace, and resiliency. In essence, our contemplative time provides us with the fuel to sustain us as we participate in our most profound practice: engaging in life in meaningful ways. This notwithstanding, the vast majority of our time is spent in our daily activities, not on a meditation cushion. Our time on a cushion, used wisely, can help us clarify and attend to our lives in healthy, productive, and meaningful ways. However, if we constantly go to the cushion to find refuge and somehow expect the mental afflictions in our lives to magically change, we'll likely be disappointed. The great wisdom teachers of the contemplative traditions constantly remind us that our primary practice is not on a cushion—it is how we treat ourselves and each other, and how we respond to the challenges that arise.

Values List

A

Acceptance
Accomplishment
Accountability
Achievement
Acknowledgment
Activism
Adaptability
Adventure
Altruism
Ambition
Appreciation
Assertiveness
Attentiveness
Awareness

B

Balance
Beauty
Being the best
Belonging
Benevolence
Bravery

C

Calmness
Camaraderie
Candor
Care
Charity
Cheerfulness
Comfort
Commitment
Community
Compassion
Competence
Competitiveness
Concentration
Confidence
Conformity
Connection
Consciousness
Consistency
Contentment
Continuous improvement
Conviction
Cooperation

Courage
Courtesy
Creativity
Credibility
Curiosity

D
Decisiveness
Democracy
Dependability
Determination
Devotion
Dignity
Diligence
Discipline
Discretion
Diversity
Drive
Duty

E
Ease
Effectiveness
Empathy
Enjoyment
Enthusiasm
Equality
Ethics

F
Fairness
Faith
Family
Fearlessness
Fidelity
Freedom
Friendliness
Fun

G
Generosity
Goodness
Grace
Gratitude
Growth

H
Happiness
Hard work
Helpfulness
Holiness
Honesty
Hopefulness
Humility
Humor

I
Impartiality
Inclusiveness
Independence
Individuality
Inner harmony
Inquisitiveness

Insightfulness
Integrity
Intelligence
Intimacy
Introspection
Intuitiveness

J
Joy
Justice

K
Kindness

L
Leadership
Legacy
Love
Loyalty

M
Making a difference
Merit
Motivation

N
Noncomformity

O
Obedience
Open-mindedness
Optimism
Order
Originality

P
Passion
Patience
Peacefulness
Perseverance
Playfulness
Power
Prudence
Punctuality

R
Rationality
Reasonableness
Relaxation
Reliability
Reputation
Resilience
Resolve
Resourcefulness
Respect
Responsibility
Restraint
Reverence

S
Self-actualization
Self-respect
Selflessness
Sensitivity
Serenity
Service
Sharing
Simplicity
Sincerity
Skillfulness
Spontaneity
Stability
Status
Stillness
Success

T
Teamwork
Temperance
Thoroughness
Thoughtfulness
Tolerance
Traditionalism
Trustworthiness
Truth

U
Uniqueness
Usefulness

V
Virtuous
Vitality

W
Willingness
Wisdom
Wonder
Worthiness